SUNSHINE and WEALTH
LOS ANGELES IN THE TWENTIES AND THIRTIES

SUNSHINE and WEALTH

LOS ANGELES IN THE TWENTIES AND THIRTIES

Bruce Henstell

Chronicle Books • San Francisco

For Pam, With Love

Library of Congress Cataloging in Publication Data.

Henstell, Bruce.
  Sunshine and wealth.
  Includes index.
  1. Los Angeles (Calif.)—Social life and customs. 2. Los Angeles (Calif.)—Popular culture. I. Title.
F869.L85H46 1984 979.4′94052 84-17595
ISBN 0-87701-275-X (pbk.)

EDITING:
Anita Keys

ART DIRECTION:
Jim Heimann

COVER & BOOK DESIGN:
Paul Mussa

COVER ILLUSTRATION:
Robert Rodriguez

Chronicle Books
870 Market Street
San Francisco,
California 94102

PHOTO CREDITS:
Collection of the author, pages: 10 left, 12, 13, 14, 15, 16, 17, 23 left, 24 above left, 25, 26, 27, 28, 30, 37, 39, 44, 46, 51, 52, 53, 55, 56, 63, 66, 71, 72, 76, 77 left, 78 above, 79, 84, 87, 91, 96, 97, 98, 100, 102, 103, 104, 105, 106, 107 above left, 108, 111, 112, 113, 114, 119 below, 125 below, 126 below, 128, 129

Collection of Richard and Nadine Hathaway, pages: 34, 38

Courtesy of Huntington Library and Botanical Gardens, San Marino, CA, pages: 18, 68

Courtesy of Los Angeles Chamber of Commerce, pages: 77 right, 82, 92 below, 93, 107 below

Courtesy of University Research Library, Department of Special Collections, University of California at Los Angeles, page: 78 below

Courtesy of *Daily News* Collection, Department of Special Collections, University Research Library, UCLA, pages: 8, 10 right, 21, 23 right, 24 above right and below, 36, 43, 48, 50, 54, 61, 64, 67, 70, 86, 88, 92 above, 94, 107 above right, 118, 119 above left and right, 120, 122 left, 123 right, 124 above, 125 above, 126 above

Courtesy of Department of Special Collections, University of Southern California, pages: 62, 116, 121, 122 right, 123 left, 124 below

ACKNOWLEDGEMENTS
  Preparing acknowledgements is a pleasure when one is lucky enough to have as many good friends and helpful associates as I am. First, once again thanks to my editor Anita Keys who has struggled to save me from myself. I am indebted to my friend and mentor Hilda Bohem, an endless source of good ideas, and all our friends at the Department of Special Collections, UCLA Research Library, including Kayla Landesman, Pearl Rosenfeld, Dan Luckenbill, and Jim Davis. I am indebted as well to Robert Knutson, director, and Ned Comstock, librarian, at the Department of Special Collections at USC Library. I'd also like to thank: Bettye Ellison and her staff at the Los Angeles Public Library; Richard and Nadine Hathaway; Joe Blackstock of Foster and Kleiser; Alan Jutzi of the Huntington Library; Cathy Auth and the Los Angeles Chamber of Commerce; Mary Anne Dolan and Leslie Ward of the *Los Angeles Herald-Examiner*; Joan Perkal; Mike Hamilburg; Hynda Rudd of the Los Angeles City Archives; Tom Vinetz; and Joe Triano for his knowledge of restaurants and boxing. For book design, I thank Jim Heimann. Finally, a special thanks to all of my friends at "Two on the Town" at KCBS television, especially executive producer Joel Tator whose good wishes and support have been more important to me than he knows.

CONTENTS

Table of Contents

Preface   7

1. There's Nothing to Stop the City of Los Angeles
   but the Ocean (and That's a Long Way Off)   13

2. God Bless the Tourist, or, All Year (and Then Some)   19

3. Folks, Have You Got Your Ticket?—Oil   31

4. Picking the Public Pocket and Other Related
   Forms of Equally Profitable Enterprise   45

5. Prohibition, or, What You Might Call the Saddest Night of All   57

6. Sportive Games and Other Amusements Afloat: The Gambling Ships   65

7. Glamorous Hollywood: The Home of the Stars and Everyone Else   73

8. Chinatown: The Mysterious East Meets the Equally Mysterious West   89

9. Sister Aimee Semple McPherson and Her Guaranteed, Sure-fire Headlines   95

10. How to Go Everywhere in the World without
    Leaving Home: Tijuana, Catalina, and Venice   99

11. What's for Breakfast? Lunch? Dinner?   109

12. The Sports Capital of the Known Universe   117

Index   130

PREFACE

The book you are about to read is your guide to the pleasures, delights and joys of Los Angeles, California, as they were experienced by tourists and residents alike between 1919 and 1939. Why the '20s and '30s? There may have been a better period in the city's history, but I doubt it.

A Californio, one of our honored ancestors of mixed Spanish/Mexican ancestry, might have said that the best days, the real good times, were back in the 1830s and 1840s, before most of the Americans had arrived. Not before *all* the Americans, the Californio would have admitted, since the first arrivals helped enliven the city. But the good times were the days before a tidal wave of immigration swept away the older culture.

In the '20s and '30s, there were a few old-timers around who would have insisted that the good times came and went with the 1890s. In those days, the sun shone all the time. A man could walk out of his downtown office after mid-morning coffee and, before long, find himself knee deep in a field of wildflowers. Orange groves were everywhere and, on warm nights, the air was heavy with their scent. Snow-capped mountains, seemingly close enough to touch, were daily visitors, as familiar a sight as the stately old Wolfskill palm tree that graced the old Southern Pacific Railroad terminal on Alameda. The first typical Southern Californian manifestation any newly arrived Easterner saw, in time the old tree was named the city's official palm. The '90s were peaceful times.

But if the Californio and the old-timer argued about which were the best times, they would have agreed that, for good times, there was no place quite like Los Angeles. The Brazilians say that their country is so beautiful it proves God must be a Brazilian. Although uncertain about the good Lord's citizenship, local Los Angeles residents took it as a matter of course that He loved their city best of all His creations.

The problems in paradise began as the word got around and the basin started to fill up. The wildest predictions about population growth started coming true. A smart man could get himself a reputation as a prophet simply by selecting some improbable number out of thin air and announcing it. Inevitably his number was reached.

At first this was fun. There was a celebration when it was announced, in mid-1920, that Los Angeles had finally outstripped San Francisco to become California's largest city. Here was retribution for a century of patronizing abuse. Later in the '20s, first USC and then UCLA demonstrated that neither Stanford nor Cal were invulnerable on the football field. And, in cultural affairs, the balance shifted as well. In 1919, William Andrews Clark founded the Los Angeles Philharmonic and the city became only the third in American history to have two symphonic organizations simultaneously. San Francisco wasn't one of the other two. Before long, San Francisco's notable conductor Alfred Hertz was summering in Los Angeles for the Hollywood Bowl season. They had nothing like the Hollywood Bowl in San Francisco. According to some good accounts, they didn't even have a summer.

About the time USC was defeating Cal for the third straight year, the pleasure of counting Los Angeles' house was starting to pale. The city

Moving in day at the *Daily News*.
C. W. Vanderbilt, Jr. is seated at
center, on top of the truck.

had outgrown its toddler's outfit, or escaped its guards, depending on which point of view you accepted. Civic leaders were untroubled by all the growth, preferring to ignore the difficulties it presented. There wasn't much in the way of planning going on. Even after the worst could be seen gathering on the horizon, dedicated city boosters treated even the act of thinking about alternatives as tantamount to civic treason. In Los Angeles, everybody was encouraged to dwell upon pleasant matters, to think about the good times.

To think about how, as a result of the boom of the '20s, a lot of people were getting rich. Los Angeles had been periodically swept by booms. Oil and real estate and Hollywood and tourism were the cars on this gravy train and it looked like there was a seat for everybody. Certainly there was an ocean of promoters and operators promising exactly that. Why, any fool could see there were more ways to make money in Los Angeles than there were to skin a cat, and many did.

When, in the 1920s, Los Angeles became one of the major oil fields in the world, a lot of ordinary folks started making a lot of money. The stories were nothing short of miraculous. And they were true. For example, everybody knew that, in the early days, folks in the East and Midwest had been offered a deed to a sliver of land in Huntington Beach with each and every encyclopedia they purchased. Unfortunately as it turned out, the buyers of what were known as the "encyclopedia lots" learned their land wasn't quite as close to the ocean as the book agents had promised. That was the bad news. The good news was that the land turned out to be saturated with oil. If sudden wealth could befall someone silly enough to buy an encyclopedia, it could happen to anybody.

One cautionary tale. Armour Phillips was broke, newly married and recently separated from the military when, immediately after the war, he decided to stake a claim in Los Angeles. He turned to sales, becoming a commission man in oil stocks. He made some money which, unfortunately, he chose to spend on a lady not his wife. When the lady who was his wife learned this, she dispatched her rival, using a hammer, to a place with more angels than even Los Angeles. The case had intense popular interest, entertainment and even amusement. Poor Armour had trouble reading the hand fate had dealt him. "Prosperity ruined us, I guess," he remarked, dazed. There is a moral here.

Whatever you make the moral out to be, please note it now. It is the last one you'll encounter. Morals were not generally appreciated in Los Angeles where good times were the order of the day. And good times don't require morals.

Morals are the result of reflection, and times were passing much too fast for that in Los Angeles. In the '20s and '30s, there were no less than six major daily newspapers being published from which flowed an endless stream of gossip, rumor, comment and even, occasionally, news which was incomprehensible by any one person on a daily basis. Life moved fast even if traffic did not.

The newspapers have been an invaluable source in the account that follows in giving a sense of how fast, how visceral, life was. The two major dailies were Harry Chandler's *Times* and W. R. Hearst's *Examiner* and they solidly hated each other. The *Examiner* took every opportunity to blast the *Times'* monopoly over the city. The *Times* usually referred to its rival as the "Examinure."

One newspaper existed in the cracks between these two giants, grabbing at the stories, the crumbs, which fell from their hands: the *Daily News*. And to the *Daily News* this book owes a special debt.

In 1920, the man described as a "millionaire reporter for the *New York Times*" published in the *Los Angeles Times* his impressions of our city. Cornelius Vanderbilt, Jr., scion of one of America's wealthiest families, was duly impressed with the "climate, scenery, the magnificent treatment . . . which draw one back to the city where there is everlasting sunshine."

This was just the sort of informed, unprejudiced commentary the *Los Angeles Times* loved to publish. The newspaper was not so accommodating when, three years later, Vanderbilt re-

EYES OF YOUR NEWSPAPER—The young men who mirror the city's life for the Illustrated Daily News. Front row, left to right: Earl Barlow, Arch Dunning and Edward Pierce. Rear row, left to right: Sid Mautner, Hiram Melvin, J. B. Scott, Teddy Hoff, Joseph A. Mingo, Peter Rowe and Marvin Spafford.

—L. A. Museum Photo.

The first stalwarts who manned the *Daily News* photo desk. Their speed, fortitude and occasionally their gall knew no bounds, but to them we are duly grateful. **Right.** Their offices at Pico and Los Angeles streets.

turned to Los Angeles, this time to start an opposition newspaper.

Vanderbilt fancied himself a populist and his newspaper, he announced, would take the workingman's side. It would cost only one penny, would feature photographs laid out in tabloid style but without the emphasis on sex and violence that New York tabloid journalism had come to rely upon. To put this shining example of virtuous journalism on the street, Vanderbilt unwittingly hired "the most riotous gang of hellraisers ever assembled under one roof," according to one chief hellraiser, *Daily News* reporter and later columnist Matt Weinstock.

The odds were against the diminutive *Daily News* in its battle against the gargantuan *Times* and *Examiner*. But, it so happened that the gods of journalism smiled upon the new baby's birthday and gave it a scoop, the biggest scoop in years — the report of the disastrous Tokyo earthquake. So the first *Daily News* hit the streets with blaring headlines which completely escaped the giants. The staff of the *News*, delirious with this success, sent out for a case of bootleg gin and proceeded to get roaring drunk. Lockstep in chain-gang style, they marched through the new newspaper's offices chanting "*Daily News! Daily News!* First on the street, got the *Examiner* and the *Times* beat!" It was the first big scoop the

Daily News got but, regrettably for those among her staff who loved the scrappy newcomer, it was also the last. In the late 1920s, the paper floundered.

It was rescued from devastation by a former *Times* ad executive, Manchester Boddy. Placed on a firmer if not really solid footing, the *Daily News* continued on until 1954 as the only mildly liberal voice in a conservative town.

For most of its life, the *Daily News* relished a good photo almost as much as a good story. The photo staff was even more uninhibited than the editorial side, if Matt Weinstock is to be believed. The first picture editor had been an officer in the French Foreign Legion and was given to wearing spats and carrying a cane. The ten photographers who served under him were uncontrollable and could, Weinstock recalled, "terrorize everyone with flash powder which after the explosion filled the vicinity with throat-searing smoke."

The photographers labored in obscurity, even more obscurity than that traditionally accorded reporters. But they succeeded in recording a view of Los Angeles now long gone but, while it lasted, joyously lived.

Much of their work, fortunately, survives. Several years ago, I became aware that the remains of the old *Daily News* had eventually come

to rest at the Department of Special Collections in UCLA's University Research Library. What survived were the original negatives. The problem was that, unless properly conserved, they would not last and, additionally, negatives are difficult for most people to work with. Together with Hilda Bohem, the Department's librarian in charge of photographic matters, a plan was developed and submitted to the National Endowment for the Humanities which saw fit to approve it. We had two goals. First was to take certain steps to help the collection survive. Second, I would review all the negatives and select 10 percent, about 20,000, which would be printed. These materials are now available at UCLA.

This book has a number of photographs from the *Daily News* collection. Many were never actually published in the paper. Some were taken on slow news days. Ironically, I doubt if any of the paper's photographers or editors realized how valuable these materials would become, what an important and interesting insight into the life of the city they provide. I thank the men (and at least one woman) who took these photographs.

What these photographs capture is Los Angeles at her best, when she was all dressed up, the skies clear, and wildflowers and orange groves everywhere. Los Angeles when the sun really did shine every day, wealth wasn't hard to come by, and good times were had by all.

A Word About Money. The gargantuan sounding sums of yesterday don't seem quite so imposing nowadays and inflation is to blame. There's been so much of it since the 1920s and 1930s that not only isn't a dollar worth a dollar but $100,000 is almost small change. For the 1920s, figure that every dollar mentioned would be worth $5 to $6 today. For the 1930s, that figure is about $4 to $5.

In Los Angeles, everybody read the
Daily News.

A tourist-eye view of Los Angeles in
the mid-1920s, the kind of snapshot
that, when it got back to Kansas or
Iowa, set tongues to wagging and lips
to smacking.

1

THERE'S NOTHING TO STOP THE CITY OF LOS ANGELES BUT THE OCEAN (AND THAT'S A LONG WAY OFF)

To the Editor: After winding through 2,165 miles of desert and mountain drives, the fields and unequaled system of highways, reached this side of the plank road over the sand hills spreading over the rural environs of Los Angeles and associated cities. It's proved to be a grand oasis in the great American desert. Its grandeur and productiveness seem not to have been overdone in publicity. Signed, Herb Lewis.

The Los Angeles dream: a home of your own. This one was located in Sherman, which ended up being called West Hollywood, ca 1923.

The Great War ended and the Great Migration began. Out of the Midwestern farms, out of the dreary industrial cities of the East, across the plains, and over the deserts they came, a trek if not overly perilous at least laborious. Onward, ever onward into the sunset they journeyed, into what the advertising said was the land of ultimate fascination and promise, Los Angeles, California. What dream drove them? The promise of sunshine and wealth: for here was the new, antiseptic Golconda, accessible via the Southern Pacific or by what they came to call the Lincoln Highway. At the end of the rainbow was Oz in an orange grove along with a white cottage and a detached garage with a late model Ford. What more was there to life? Not much.

In August, 1919, 21,000 persons give or take a few entered Los Angeles by train, automobile and steamship. In August, 1920, Los Angeles incredulously realized that this figure had doubled and, only a few months later, the total had broken 60,000 and was still climbing. More startling was that among these folks were a lot who were here to stay and not passing through. "It is no longer a question of whether people are going to Southern California," the Assistant General Traffic Manager of the highly delighted Santa Fe told Los Angeles, "but whether you will be able to handle them when they get there. They are simply going to go that way in droves... and a large portion are planning to stay."

When the government counted noses in 1920, there were slightly more than 900,000 souls resident in the county, and when that exercise was repeated in 1930, there were slightly more than 2,200,000. Which meant that, on average, slightly more than 350 folks permanently settled here each and every day during the decade. And there was nothing slight about such an internal migration.

The map of Los Angeles erupted, producing Torrance, Tujunga, South Gate, Lynwood, Bell, Hawthorne, Maywood and more in addition to a handful of other towns that graduated into cities. "They camped on the outskirts of town," wrote one observer, "and their camps became new suburbs." People in Riverside or Ventura, who'd moved there for the rural isolation, feared they

-In the Center of West Los Angeles District-

At the time this promotional brochure was issued, Sawtelle was an independent city. Before long it was just another neighborhood of Los Angeles, to which it was annexed.

would no longer have to go into Los Angeles: Los Angeles would move out to them.

The changes this growth brought were neither slow nor subtle and struck L.A. residents right between the eyes, particularly those who had been here a few years already and were practically natives. "Where are the citrus and olive groves, the vineyards and friendly flower gardens by the side of the road of yesteryear that made excursions into the suburbs of Los Angeles the joy of joys?" breathlessly questioned one old newcomer. "Now Southern California is varicolored, principally yellow with sordid shacks, dust, disorder and landscape-defacing billboards. What a melancholy contrast—an agricultural, horticultural, artistic gem transformed into a medley of hideous things." This was in 1923. The best, or worst, was yet to come.

"SUBDIVISION ACTIVITY BREAKS PAST RECORD" was a headline repeated in the *Record,* the *Express,* the *Examiner* and especially in the *Times,* chief booster of the only occasionally comprehensible boom which was underway. "Architects and builders look for no letup in local building activities,"—1920. "Another banner year is already in sight,"—1922. In 1919, building permits worth $28 million were issued. That became $60 million in 1920, $121 million in 1921 and $200 million in 1923. Investment on this scale meant something was being built just about all the time, just about everywhere in the city.

Between November, 1921, when the city engineer first took official notice of subdivisions, and November, 1922, 631 new subdivisions were considered, 47 in one record-breaking month. Which meant that the old City Hall on Broadway was awash with harried bureaucrats confronting, treadmill style, increasingly impatient businessmen. When the *City Directory* for 1922 appeared, Los Angeles realized it had gained 60,822 listings for one year. Between Mr. J. Herman Aagard, the first name listed, and Nicodemus Zyhlinska, a blacksmith and the last named, the *Directory* carried 2,292 pages, 253 more than the previous year.

In 1920, there were more than 100 lumber

schooners in Los Angeles harbor unloading 90 million board feet of timber each month, where the prewar high had been a modest 5–6 million feet. The L.A. construction industry was devouring this fodder and spewing it out as 1,500 new houses each month. Not atypical was the claim of Ferguson Construction at mid-decade that it had built, plastered and stuccoed a new home on Whittier Boulevard in a record ten days, start to finish.

"In every part of the city one may see dwellings in the course of construction," intoned the *Times,* "and rapidly Los Angeles is being built up solidly in the direction of the sea, and the Hollywood Hills, as well as to the south and east." The poppy fields and the inland seas of goldenrod and mustard grass began disappearing, replaced by cottages, apartment buildings and bungalow courts which crept across the face of the city as if the gods were playing Monopoly.

Nothing was permanent in the geography of Los Angeles. When Wilshire reached West Lake, instead of skirting around it, Los Angeles parted the waters and the lake was cut in two. Around Third, Vermont and Wilshire was a swamp. Springs there fed the Bimini Baths. In the late 1920s, developers began filling in the area and eventually the slough that had been there became a dim memory.

"To the Editor: There was a question a few days ago about having skyscrapers in Los Angeles. The skyscrapers we have are the direct and primary cause of the congestion. Why make things worse by building more? If the buildings were lower and more spread out over more territory so would traffic be more spread out and there is certainly plenty of room for this city to spread: there is nothing to stop Los Angeles but the ocean and it is quite a way off." Signed, Reader.

"In a few years, the farseeing experts say Los Angeles will reach solidly from the mountains to the sea with all remaining acreage tracts subdivided and built up," commented the *Times* in 1920. Yes, and "Los Angeles will stop buying lots," added one realtor, "when there are no

The Belvedere Gardens Square subdivision in East Los Angeles, showing that at least at first everything didn't look as nice as advertised.

more to sell." That, dear Reader, was that.

"From grain field to thriving community," read a 1922 account of Culver City. "To appreciate Culver City . . . it is necessary to go back to the time when the townsite was nothing more than a field of grain on which a real estate man held an option." The rest, and the story was repeated endlessly, was history. All the grain got shoved aside and in its place were planted two banks, two newspapers, five churches, a hospital and the Venice line of the Pacific Electric though, in fairness, that was there before there was a Culver City and that that was the case was a good reason why there was a Culver City at all.

Another reason was Harry H. Culver, born in Nebraska, graduate of the school of real estate subdivision taught by I. N. Van Nuys when that worthy owned and subdivided a large portion of the San Fernando valley. Harry Culver was short and nondescript although at times he resembled his contemporary—the ill-fated screen comedian, Harry Langdon. Culver was devoid of self-doubt, possessed of inexhaustible reserves of go-get-itness, and the kind of man his peers and the press loved to call a dreamer, who "first dreamed of the possibilities of a grain field."

Harry Culver knew a secret and it was, as he put it, that "what seems to attract people is something moving." So you never caught Harry Culver standing still. He installed an 800,000-watt searchlight on the roof of his sales office, staged polo games between Ford Model Ts, gave a building lot to "Culver City's most beautiful baby," and gifted a local druggist with an around-the-world cruise for coming up with the name for a new subdivision. The winning entry, Media Park, seems unremarkable, but that didn't matter. It brought him the names of 50,000 new prospects. Unsatisfied with his natural gifts, Culver hired a vocal coach and worked out like some athlete in an empty movie theater. At one point his company was building cottages, stocking them with every imaginable household appliance down to dishes and glassware, landscaping the grounds, putting the car in the garage, everything: "So completely that one might step in and

Before long, Harry Culver's Culver City looked downright respectable.

prepare a meal by only supplying the groceries." For all of this, Harry Culver was eventually elected president of the state association of real estate agents.

When the real estate conflagration was at its height, fortunes were to be made overnight. A young girl named Mary was one of those the Goddess of Development touched. What her last name was, was irrelevant. Her advertisements said that, for real estate, Los Angeles should "See Mary" and that was enough.

Mary was seventeen when she got into the business. With only $30, and that borrowed, she opened an office. She looked prosperous even if she wasn't and that's what mattered. Soon she made her first sale—a garage. Not much but a start. "That small stuff is the hardest," she remarked. "Money is magnetic you know. It is easier to sell a $10,000 piece of property than a $4,000 bungalow." Her first month's commission check was in excess of $1,000. In two years, she had amassed $30,000 in cash, "a canyon or two of

her own," and a very large limousine.

No real estate promotion was complete without a free lunch. You could eat your way through the 1920s for the price of listening to a few thousand sales pitches. Every morning, hundreds of excursion buses were on the road, filled with the curious and the hungry. Each had its spieler with a well-rehearsed presentation: "My only wish," began one, "is that you could appreciate with the same certainty that I do the good fortune in store for you. Follow my advice and buy one, or ten, of these lots, regardless of the sacrifice it might mean. Ten thousand banks may close, stocks may smash, bonds may shrink to little or nothing, but this tract and Los Angeles real estate stand like the Rock of Gibraltar for safety, certainty and profit. Don't be satisfied with 6 percent on your money. Don't be satisfied with 12 percent. Buy property like this and keep it and, as sure as the world moves, it will pay you 100 percent to 1,000 percent and more per annum. Be among those who earn from 100 percent to 10,000 percent. We offer you the opportunity . . ."

Then lunch. When a newspaper asked readers what they disliked most about Los Angeles, one reply was "the failure of oil promoters and real estate speculators to provide for their guests' breakfasts and dinner and lodging as well as lunch."

W. P. Whitsett sales managed the township of Van Nuys. He named the development Van Nuys rather than Whitsett because, as confident as he was, he wasn't certain the promotion would go over. Whitsett paid porters at the Fifth Street train station to tag the luggage of incoming visitors with passes for a free bus ride and lunch in Van Nuys. He blanketed Los Angeles with small wooden thimbles with a nail inserted in them which, when twisted, sounded vaguely like the chirping of chickens. This was a reminder that Van Nuys homesites included land enough for a little urban farming. "While the greatest social activity centered in and around Hollywood," wrote a witness to the merchandising, "suburban land owners and promoters were busy creating

Advertisement for West Van Nuys development, 1923.

acre homesites, small fruit farms and chicken ranches. As an inducement to early buyers, the promoters offered a thousand hens and a few roosters to every purchaser, with an assurance that the white leghorn route was the latest and quickest road to financial independence."

The Los Angeles Chamber of Commerce's Agricultural Department cheerily assured farm-experienced refugees from the Midwest that Los Angeles was an agrarian paradise. "The possibility of living and working in the open air and sunshine year 'round, the profitableness of farming where two or more crops a year is the rule rather than the exception . . . there is no other part of the country where there are so many persons enjoying the advantages of country life with none of its hardships."

Glendale, in the early 1920s, was claiming it was the "Fastest Growing City in America." It hadn't amounted to much until 1904, when the Pacific Electric finally reached the top site of the old Rancho San Rafael. Developer Leslie C. Brand got going and Glendale was incorporated in 1906, just in time: "The question of where to live in suburban happiness and at the same time travel daily to and from Los Angeles [was] solved." Glendale began to "widen like a rain-fed pool," an ill-chosen image since it never rained in Southern California. There were 2,742 people in residence by 1910, 60,000 by 1925 — 10,000 of which had appeared in the previous twelve months. Why? Because it had "lovely canyons and by-paths of friendly mountains," twelve grammar schools, two high schools, six hotels and "a strictly white population . . . There are not a half dozen other than Caucasians [in the schools]." Pacific Electric trains ran to Los Angeles every thirty minutes, buses were available to Pasadena, Hollywood and Santa Monica, and there were five automobile boulevards close by, three to Los Angeles. Why it was impossible not to taste Glendale's success when a propagandist wrote: "Nature gave Glendale the brooding hills and the sun-swept valley. . . . But where man has so often taken a prospect that pleases and made it vile through his own unimaginative soul, the builders of Glendale have been partners with beauty and lovers of the immaculate, to the end that today one may look upon this remarkable municipal achievement and renew faith that the necessity for the practical has not altogether clouded the artistic vision of the American people."

Hollywood was an old community. The real estate promoters who rediscovered the area called it, "Los Angeles' Palatial Residential District . . . If you own a lot or home in Hollywood, you can go to sleep at night satisfied that it will hold its value as something substantial based upon real value." Real, genuine, down to earth. "There is the education story," a promotional brochure vouchsafed, "of a young couple that bought a few acres in Hollywood and, soon after they were married, went abroad for a year, returned, and found that the land had risen $10,000 during their absence. They sold part, took their profit and started to spend the money, came back in another year to find that what was left of the land had advanced $10,000 more, paying for all their trip and leaving a handsome profit, and this sort of delightful endless chain of rising values is not uncommon . . ."

Endorsing these values was not just a movie star. The promoters of Hollywood called upon none other than L. Frank Baum, beloved author of *The Wizard of Oz,* who testified that he and his wife referred to Hollywood as "the land of enchantment . . . [We had] passed a winter on the Nile, another at beautiful Taormina, had wintered at Sorrento, at Nice, and, in America, at the Florida and gulf coast resorts. But it is only after we discovered Hollywood . . . that we wandered no more."

The PE tried to keep up with the demand for service via fixed rails but, before long, it was clearly a hopeless case. In expanding routes in the late 1920s, the PE went into the bus business.

2

GOD BLESS THE TOURIST, OR, ALL YEAR (AND THEN SOME)

To the All-Year Club: We have always spent our summers motoring through New England. We had always imagined Southern California would be too hot to visit in the summer time. We are going to try it this year.

According to long-time newspaper columnist Matt Weinstock, the realization that Los Angeles of all places had a weather problem occurred in the following manner. At the conclusion of World War I, inflation hit the city. The *Times* took to printing the names of those whose prices caused them to be suspected of gouging the tourist trade. One lady who found her name in the paper charged into the office of editor Harry Chandler and insisted she had to charge more during the winter tourist months to cover her expenses during the summer when no tourists appeared. Impressed with what she had to say, Harry called some friends together and the All-Year Club was the result.

If the city had somehow gotten the reputation for having unbearable summers, that was a misunderstanding that had to be corrected. The Club's big advertising ploy was its statement: "It is even possible to guarantee summer visitors that they will sleep under blankets at least nine nights out of every ten that they spend in Southern California." Or, to let the United States Weather Bureau tell the story: "This Southern portion of California is blessed with the fairest weather the year 'round that is to be found in any section of the Union."

The All-Year Club was no sedate public relations office. Funded by the county government and interested businessmen, it functioned like a ministry of information, its basement engines working overtime to get out the message that Los Angeles was the most favored spot on earth. Beginning with a modest $40,000 budget in 1921, the Club told the world: "No ordinary vacation will do — *this* summer. You've earned, you need, a *real* vacation." Next came the "Nights under blankets" promotion. And twice each year thereafter, the Club developed a new theme in its ceaseless drumming of the good life to be experienced in Los Angeles: health ("A new man in two weeks!"); cost ("$70 for 11 days in California!"); climate ("Exchange your winter for the smiles of spring"). In the 1920s, Club advertisements were appearing in 50 daily and 20 Sunday newspapers. By 1930, that was up to 79 dailies. In 1926 alone, the Club contacted 12 million people, and 800 to 1,500 of those personally visited the Club's headquarters on West Adams each day. The Club missed no trick. Thousands of photographs were supplied gratis to newspapers across the country. More than 2,000 copies of the publication *Pictorial California* were sent each month to travel agents.

Was there a literate individual anywhere in the Western World who hadn't heard about Los Angeles? Unlikely, since the Club estimated it reached 272 million people each year. The Club's initial budget had multiplied many times over. And tourism had, by the early 1930s, grown to be Southern California's second biggest industry.

And what the Club left undone the Chamber of Commerce promptly attacked. The C of C sponsored exhibits, including entire special trains, which toured the country visiting exhibitions and fairs. The Chamber maintained a full-time Chautauqua lecturer. Energetic president Frank Wiggins, an invalid who'd moved West to die and who had been miraculously cured, decided everybody must know of Los Angeles. His friend, engineer William Mulholland, commented that the only way to stop the growth of Los Angeles was to kill Frank Wiggins. But his unexpected, albeit natural, death in 1924 did nothing to slow the upturn in population.

In 1924, L.A.'s propaganda machine nearly slipped a cog. Two events, acts of God, were visited upon Los Angeles. First, there was an outbreak of bubonic plague in Sonoratown, the city's poor, Mexican district. Next, and far more serious, was a state-wide outbreak of anthrax, "hoof and mouth" disease as it was called. Since Los Angeles was the nation's number one agricultural county and since a lot of the people Los Angeles was trying to attract spoke the language of agriculture, this was serious indeed. The public parks had to be closed as a precaution and the dedication of a new club house at the Griffith Park golf course postponed. Cattle were slaughtered to check the spread of the disease. In Lankershim, the Fred Hartsook herd was wiped out, including such champions as Tillie Alcarta and Sir Aagie De Kol Meade. All roads out of the state were guarded day and night and disinfec-

tion of cargos demanded. Eventually 2 percent of the state's herds were lost. The disease abated but the damage had been done.

Los Angeles was outraged at the reaction of critics to all this adversity. Some critics not only reported these misfortunes but gloated over them as blemishes on the squeaky-clean face Los Angeles advertising presented to the world. Humorless local correspondents shot back that Eastern naysaying wasn't just an effrontery. "Propagandists who seek to accomplish stagnation in any of the great producing territories," wrote one newspaper, "are guilty of constructive treason to the entire nation."

Los Angeles was paradise and anyone who stood in the way of the rush here was mean indeed. With one picturesque exception — an episode which, in the early 1930s, became known as the Bum Blockade. In that incident, Los Angeles tried to restrict immigration as resolutely and creatively as it had tried previously to promote it.

Early on, city fathers realized that California attracted as many, to their minds, undesirables as it did good citizens, i.e. those with pockets full of cash to invest. In Chamber publications at the turn of the century, people were warned not to come unless they had funds, since jobs, particularly unskilled and semiskilled, were hard to come by. It got worse during the 1920s and, in 1929, the mayor warned that "the attractiveness of our climate created a winter unemployment situation . . . which is never easy to meet."

The city implored the state legislature to do something about the influx of vagrants. Harry Carr, the *Times* columnist who wrote under the name "Lancer," and who had been a reporter in China, suggested good roads were the problem, and that the Chinese "wiser than we, have delayed building a great system of highways to head off these dangerous migrations."

James E. "Two Gun" Davis, the city's spit and polish police chief, had a solution. It was to post men at the border and deny entry to those who didn't have liquid assets. It was doubtless an idea born of the auto blockades staged within the

James Edgar Davis, twice police chief of Los Angeles, earned the sobriquet Two Gun owing to his extraordinary pistol marksmanship. Davis ardently supported the LAPD's target-shooting team which was known around the world.

there had been a dramatic decrease in crime. The *Times* supported the blockade eloquently.

The All-Year Club was caught in the middle and, embarrassed by the blockade, tried to ignore it. In an internal memorandum, the Club related one local businessman's word that "Chief Davis is doing a wonderful thing in stopping transients at the border." But, the businessman worried, he had had a letter from a friend back East who owned a $22,000 house and who wondered if he would be stopped at the border. The solution the businessman had to offer was "increased financial support to the All-Year Club . . . to offset the misconstruction which Eastern states are placing on our border activities."

The most famous case associated with the Bum Blockade was that of mining man and former motion picture director John Langan. He had been working in Arizona and, when he tried to cross back into California still wearing his dirty clothes, the LAPD turned him around. He was angry enough to file suit against Chief Davis. But when the suit came before a Federal judge, Langan suddenly asked it be dropped. He had a change of heart he said. His surprised counsel insisted the change of heart had come after police harassment of both Langan and his wife. The man who seems to have presented the police point of view personally to Langan was Lieutenant Earl E. Kynette, who was later sent to San Quentin for planting a bomb in an effort to discourage an investigation of official corruption. The case was sticky indeed, generated considerable ill press for the Department, and eventually helped convince the LAPD to fight crime closer to home.

The truth is that, even among those who did get into the promised land, there were some who found it wanting in minor respects. For example, typical is this letter to the editor published in 1924:

"There is so much talk about the riches of Los Angeles that folks back East think you can find money lying in the streets here. I have come from Kentucky and find matters quite different. If I had not been an auto mechanic I could not

city, where officers routinely questioned and inspected all cars for little or no reason. Davis voiced the opinion that the purpose of such searches was to halt crime and that law-abiding citizens would welcome them.

Los Angeles city policemen were assigned to the state's far-off borders and were deputized by local authorities. All cars were halted and all persons having no "definite purpose in coming into the state" coupled with no means of support, were offered a choice: either to turn around and go back where they came from or to serve a prison term with hard labor for vagrancy.

The ACLU's reaction was predictable. It asserted that, if the Second Coming occurred, Jesus wouldn't be able to get past Davis' goons. One newspaper said the blockade "violates every principle that Americans hold dear." The LAPD was thrown out of at least one county for roughing up local citizens. Chief Davis, of course, insisted that, since the blockade had begun, have found employment. As it is now I can hardly make ends meet at the low wages I receive."

And that wasn't all. Some other complaints:

Noise. A good number of immigrants were from rural areas and just weren't used to the noise of city life. "This city could get along much better with much less noise," said one, "less shouting of newsies, screeching sirens, auto horns and clanging street car gongs." But that wasn't all. The natives objected to the immigrants' habit of bringing a little piece of the farm with them. "When will Los Angeles authorities wake up and rid us of our screaming roosters? They are not only a nuisance but a menace to health. No wonder they tell us in San Francisco, 'Go back to your village and listen all night to your roosters!' It's impossible to get a healthy night's sleep here!" Not everybody was in favor of immediate action. One reply to complaints about the roosters was that, if they were all done away with simultaneously, it would flood the market with tough birds.

Dress. It was hard with all the sunshine to dress formally. One newcomer mused about the citizens of Los Angeles: "I wonder if more than a dozen men in all California own dress suits? The men back East would be ashamed to dress in that rough way." What could you do about a place where, when the Los Angeles County Employees' Association gathered for its annual dance and card party in the Goldberg-Bosley assembly rooms the invitation insisted "wear your old clothes and be happy." Denim struck Los Angeles in the early 1920s. Judges wore it, Fatty Arbuckle wore it, students at Hollywood High went in for striped denim. Why not, when suits were going for between $50 and $150.

Cults. "The legend," wrote columnist Matt Weinstock, "is that Los Angeles is a hastily thrown together smear of pink and blue stucco doll houses, inhabited by long-haired men and short-haired women, clairvoyants, swamis, herb doctors, chiropractors, nature lovers, depraved motion-picture actors, psychopathic murderers, painless dentists, bond salesmen, gunmen, winos, radio announcers and people who open every conversation with 'what's doin'?' " True.

Local resident Dr. Carl A. Wickland, author of *Thirty Years Among the Dead,* head of the National Psychological Institute on Hayes Avenue, conducted seances employing his wife who was in constant communication with the beyond through her spirit guide, a little Indian girl named Silver Star. Almost all cases of insanity were, according to Dr. Wickland, attributable to spirit possession, the spirits unaware that they were actually dead. This also accounted for the number of haunted houses.

The spiritual beliefs of A. E. Press were more down to earth. He operated a kind of commune on Willowbrook which practiced sunshine, cold water and nudity. The neighbors assented to the first two. "I have no religion," he told the press, "no country, no creed except nature. I am a child of the Universe."

When the most fabled quack of his generation, Dr. J. R. Brinkley of Kansas came through town, he was well received. Dr. Brinkley had developed the technique of surgically implanting in the male scrotum goat gland tissue. Why? Everybody knew how virile goats were. The doctor was requested to open a branch of his operation here. "I expect to return," he said. "The gland operations cannot be performed in the summer months in Kansas because of the heat. Here we could find a location near Los Angeles where we could operate the year 'round." Another advantage of the Southern California climate.

"It seems to me that the medical laws of the state must be very lax," remarked one resident. "I have never heard of so many 'ists' in all my life until I came to California." Another visitor observed: "Everybody here has his own idea about the here and the hereafter. If people would spend a little more time trying to live in this life and not worry so much about the life to come, they would be better off."

Lawn Sprinklers. A serious problem in the brave new world where everybody had his own front lawn and was proud of it. "I should like to know by what authority," wrote one disgruntled

Catalina and everything in between.

The native was sure to suggest to the tourist that the best and cheapest way to see Southern California was aboard a Big Red Car. There were 6,000 trains each day over 115 different routes, and the basic fare was five cents. There was the Orange Empire Trolley Trip: Riverside, Glenwood, Mission Inn, Redlands and Smiley Heights, twice daily trains, $4.00 and lots of orange groves along the way. Or the beach cities, Hollywood and Beverly Hills along the Balloon Route. Or Mt. Lowe, five trains daily, $2.50 round trip.

In 1915, the president of the PE called Los Angeles an "electric railway paradise." It was. Graceful new cars glided over miles of unobstructed right of way, past spectacular scenery, delivering passengers in, as the company boasted on its logo, speed, safety, comfort. Yet, by 1920, for all its apparent health, the system had begun to die. Its death throes were spasmodic and ultimately irreversible.

Los Angeles was growing up too fast. There were too many people to serve and they were taking up residence in places increasingly distant from the tracks the PE operated. For example, on the west side of Los Angeles, the area of greatest growth, the PE was hopelessly behind in laying new track. The PE struggled to keep up and failed. New service was by bus. Expenses were up, the demand for new capital unceasing, and ridership was always decreasing. Before long, the PE would be forced to ask for an increase in its fares and this drove still more riders off the streetcars. It was a vicious circle that was impossible to break.

PE passengers were routinely referred to as "demoralized." Take rerouting. Periodic rerouting of the system was necessary to try and fit it to the expanding population but it inevitably angered everybody. The great rerouting of May 1920 was greeted by the following comment offered by Chief of Police George Home: "Never thought that I would lose myself in Los Angeles, but I sure did this morning. My automobile was out of order and I took a streetcar. It looked all

newcomer to a newspaper, "property owners are permitted to leave their sprinklers running unwatched, overlapping both sides of the sidewalk. This is being practiced all over the city to a degree of intolerance. Frequently it is necessary for pedestrians to resort to the street to avoid this annoyance."

The Pacific Electric. A visitor arriving in Los Angeles in the 1920s would have been immediately impressed by the size of the Pacific Electric, Southern California's streetcar system. Biggest in the world! some native was sure to boast, with 1,000 miles of track connecting cities from San Fernando to Balboa. In 1924, 109,185,650 passengers rode the rails. Via a PE Big Red Car or a Yellow Car of the Los Angeles Railway, which operated within L.A. city limits, it was only an hour from the surf at Santa Monica to downtown and another forty-five minutes to Pasadena. There was a subway, and there was Mt. Lowe, the magical incline railway behind Pasadena that lifted you up the sheer face of a mountain and then twisted around until you reached the summit and the Alpine Tavern. You could see clear to

Left. The Pacific Electric and the Los Angeles Railway tried hard to please the public, but somehow everything came up a cropper.

Right. The Toluca Yards, exit point of the first and only Los Angeles subway, at Second Street and Beverly Boulevard, ca 1939.

There just wasn't enough room on the streets for all the cars, streetcars and pedestrians and it was the last who usually came out the worst. However, some retired PE streetcars posed no danger to pedestrians.

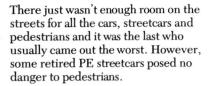

right and ran all right but it never got me to where I wanted to go. No more streetcars for me. I take an automobile or I walk." With friends such as the Chief, who needed enemies?

Hardly anyone had anything nice to say about the poor streetcars. Newspapers crusaded against the rising toll of auto–streetcar and streetcar–pedestrian accidents. To win back riders by increasing speed meant avoiding crowded streets, so, in 1924, the PE began construction of a downtown subway. The completed tunnel ran for slightly more than a mile from the Subway Terminal Building at 417 S. Hill to the Toluca Yards at Second and Beverly, where passengers could get cars to Hollywood or Glendale. Since Prohibition was on when the first train began service, it was christened not with the traditional champagne but with ginger ale. The subway was a success for all that mattered. It was unfortunately just a pale reflection of a magnificent plan for a series of tunnels and subways that had been proposed as early as 1907.

"This so-called trolley car service is getting to be a joke," one angry rider wrote her newspaper. "I did ride the Yellow Cars daily but, after standing up for months, and paying my nickels regularly, only to be packed in and jerked off and on the streetcars daily, I decided to move to this beach. The Red Cars are almost as bad."

" 'Tourist' asks why Angelenos go around looking so angry," wrote another reader. "It is because of the overcrowded streetcars. Wait until 'Tourist' has lived here long enough to use the Los Angeles Street Railway night and morning and he, too, will join the throng of angry people." Another reader had the perfect nonsolution to all the problems: "During the World War the streetcar companies cut out every other stop. During the power shortage they cut out some more. Their next move will be to have everyone walk to the end of the line, buy a through ticket to the other end, and then walk to his or her place of business."

But the root of the problem was that Los Angeles loved automobiles. People might be riding streetcars but they were thinking about auto-

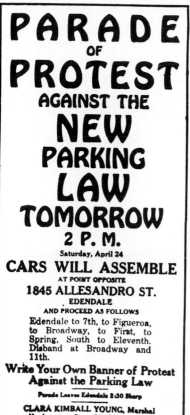

To protest the parking ban, a parade was organized. As this was a Los Angeles parade, movie star Clara Kimball Young was enlisted as Marshal.

mobiles. The elite of Los Angeles believed in the automobile. It "enabled the working man, the man of moderate means, to live a considerable distance from his work, thereby enabling him to own his own home, and to have lawns, flowers, shrubbery." The auto freed the city from the spectacle of "tenement houses or cheap apartments where living conditions tend to the certain deterioration of the races." The auto let the city dweller attend lectures and outdoor art shows and visit friends "where, in the old and tedious days of streetcar travel, such recreation and enjoyment would have been impossible."

Or, as one Los Angeles auto paint company advertised in the '20s: "You doll-up your wife, why let her ride in a shabby car?" In Los Angeles you were married to your car. And, in the process of getting a divorce from the Pacific Electric.

Traffic. Of course, once the unwary pedestrian was forced to retreat into the street to avoid soaking his pant cuffs from unattended sprinklers, he ran the risk of getting run over. Pedestrians, when they crossed the minds of Los Angeles motorists at all, did so framed by cross hairs. "Although this is the most wonderful climate and most attractive city I have ever found," remarked a lady, "yet, until some plan is devised to protect pedestrians, I must keep my children in the South. The city is losing many desirable residents because it is so difficult to cross the streets."

The traffic problem was only an outgrowth of Los Angeles' continuing fascination with the automobile. If there can be said to have been one instant, one point in time where the domination of the auto over all became complete, that moment came in April of 1920, just as the great tourist surge was beginning. To understand how that moment came about, it's necessary to look back a few years.

Autos had first begun to appear on Los Angeles' streets in the 1890s and, by 1910, the city was forced to regulate their conduct. The problem was with the "scorchers," reckless maniacs who whizzed through downtown regardless of others. It was made illegal to travel through the central city at any speed in excess of twelve miles

per hour.

By 1920, there were more than 160,000 autos in Los Angeles and nobody had to worry about the scorchers. Downtown autos challenged one another for the few precious inches of space available, traffic moved like jelly and the entire area was officially labeled a "congested area."

A side effect of the traffic mess was that the streetcars couldn't get through and so were forty-five minutes to an hour late on every run through downtown. When the Los Angeles Railway applied to the State Railroad Commission, which regulated transit systems, for a rate increase, not only did it not get it but it was ordered by the Commission to do something about getting its trains back on schedule. The Railway turned to the city and the city came up with the brilliant, innovative suggestion of banning parking from downtown during peak hours. An ordinance was drafted and passed. It went into effect with much expectation.

On enforcement eve, Captain James McDowell of the Traffic Bureau was armed with 5,000 freshly printed tickets. The honor of being the first charged with violating the new ordinance fell to James Wynne, nineteen, who refused to remove his vehicle from in front of the store in which he worked on First Street. That day, 1,000 tickets were handed out.

Magically, the streetcars began making their schedules. The mayor pronounced himself happy. The traffic engineers were happy. "After the first day of the ordinance," editorialized a newspaper, "everybody seemed satisfied . . . except the motorists, the professional men, the business houses and the police." The businessmen were particularly unhappy. Despite studies which showed the rate of pedestrian traffic was up, the merchants insisted there had been anywhere from a 20 to 50 percent drop in business.

Earle C. Anthony, a prominent downtown businessman, was so infuriated with the new ordinance that he planned a challenge to its constitutionality. After all, it clearly discriminated since it only regulated motorists, not pedestrians.

The *Times* had at first lukewarmly supported

ORT OF THE UNITED PRESS ASSOCIATIONS   COMPLETE SERVICE OF THE NEWSPAPER ENTERPRISE ASSOCIATION

Los Angeles Record   2 CENTS
EVENING EDITION

TUESDAY, APRIL 27, 1920   Number 7881

Parking Up To 4 P.M.

FOUR MORE COPS FIRED BY SNYDER

Mayor Demands Suspension By Chief.

HACKETT IS NAMED

Sergeant Acquitted In Bribery Case Attacked.

Young Slayer of Child-Bride Says Murder Ended Troubles

TRAFFIC LAW CHANGED TO SUIT STORES

Council Adopts Amended No-Parking Ordinance.

CHANGE OF HOURS

Autos Can Stand On Streets Till 4 P. M.

Huh! San Diego Air Blasts May Be Tia Juana Hiccoughs

the ordinance but, in the face of business opposition, it quickly changed its position. The newspaper cynically suggested that the city hadn't gone far enough. It had "merely deprived motorists of the rights of citizens and taxpayers and has failed to make it clear . . . that they are also outcasts, and not entitled to the reasonable privileges accorded human beings." By which was meant the God-given right to park.

A protest was planned and, since no demonstration was complete without the participation of a movie star, actress Clara Kimball Young was enlisted as grand marshal.

The city council caved in and repealed the ordinance. This despite the desperate pleas of the engineers that it had proved its workability. One man satisfied by the council's action was Gilbert Woodill, chairman of the local Motor Car Dealers Association. "It didn't take Los Angeles twenty-four hours to realize," said Woodill, "that removing the automobile from the streets meant the same thing as cutting the throat of business." The *Times* concurred. The experiment proved "Southern California throb[s] in unison with the purring motors of its automobiles." There was a lesson in all this as far as Woodill was concerned: "The sooner [the authorities] realize that hampering the use of the automobile is hampering the progress of civilization, the better off we all will be."

The city council soon caved in on the no parking ordinance, a predictable result given the alignment of forces: business vs. government.

Pronunciation. One of the severest problems the city faced was that nobody knew how to pronounce its name. A radio listener in Chicago wrote plaintively to a Los Angeles newspaper requesting clarification: "Last night two announcers at two different radio stations pronounced it two different ways. If people in Los Angeles do not know how to pronounce the name of their own town, who does?" Actually nobody did. The following was current as early as 1909:

When I came upon the bus
The Porter called 'Loss Anjy-lus!'
But others— when I talked with these—
Pronounced it thus: 'Loss Anjylese!'
A few days since a bright young miss
Surprised me with 'Las Anjy-lis!'
But, 'mongst the cultivated, one soon sees
The real thing is 'Lows Anklyese!'

The *Los Angeles Times* insisted that Angelenos were slaughtering the name of the city. Since presumably everybody heeded the voice of the *Times,* the newspaper for years ran on its editorial page, directly below the paper's masthead, this one line: "LOS ANGELES (Loce Ahng hail ais)." The *Times* said this was the Spanish pronunciation and the correct one.

In 1934, when the United States Geographical Board recognized the vernacular pronunciation, "Los An-je-less" the *Times* was outraged. This utterance made the city "sound like some brand of fruit preserve." The *Times* saw a plot, an effort by hard-headed Easterners to soften up the West Coast by getting the major metropolis there to fall for an aberrant pronunciation and, with Los Angeles (Loce Ahng hail ais) fallen, it would be "easy to bring into line the other Southern California cities which also rejoice in soft, sibilant Spanish syllables."

Would it be Sandy Ego next? La Jolla for La Hoya, San Joce, San Jokkin and Agwa Calyent? The *Times* did not choose to make note of the recognized local pronunciation of San Pedro as San Pee-dro rather than the correct Spanish pronunciation of San Pey-dro. Nor did the newspaper note that other communities across the country had anglicized their names, often to dis-

Malibu Beach, Calif.
Motion Picture Colony

If the Venice beach was too crowded on most Saturdays and Sundays and on Wednesdays, as well as all the holidays, the Malibu Colony, suburban paradise inhabited mainly by Hollywood's elite, was guaranteed to be scantly occupied. The stars discovered Malibu early. How famous was it? A shiver passed through it when Los Angeles newspapers reported the rumor that gangster Pretty Boy Floyd was planning to attack the Colony by airplane and kidnap a star.

harmonious effect. Was there a worse offender than the intersection of Gratoit (Grach-it) and Livernois (Liver-noise) in the city of Detroit?

Guide books routinely commented upon the confusion. One noted that the city's name was frequently simply abbreviated to "Los" or just "L.A." After World War I, the Navy decided to christen one of its huge dirigibles after the city. A cynic suggested that, considering all the advertising the city did, it was the only name they could give the biggest gas bag in the world.

The Beaches. The beaches were one of Los Angeles' genuine attractions. When the beaches got crowded in the 1920s and 1930s, they got crowded as they have never been crowded since. On the July 4 weekend in 1925, for example, three-car streetcar trains arrived every four minutes through the day and every one was jammed. It was literally standing room only at the beach.

It was hardly surprising that the constant complaint about the beaches was that they were dirty. "Let us clean up the beaches and keep the lunch box crowd off," said one outraged beachgoer. "Now the bathers must walk over the remains of someone's lunch."

Earthquakes. Contrary to popular preconception, there was nothing to fear hereabouts from earthquakes.

In 1920, a sharp tremor hit the city and who better to turn to for an explanation than William Mulholland, city engineer and geologist extraordinaire, if largely self-taught. Mulholland assured the city that "there was nothing to indicate there will ever be a dangerous quake here" although some dis-ease could be expected due to the nearby San Andreas fault. Engineer Bill wasn't exactly sure what the San Andreas fault was. As he knew, a fault indicated "that far under the surface of the earth something is not properly adjusted."

A survey of the records clearly showed that, while San Francisco had been rocked and rolled at least three times in historic record, Los Angeles "has never suffered damage from the few quakes which have visited the city." It was not pointed out that the last time a major quake had

visited Los Angeles (the Fort Tejon shake of 1852), there wasn't much of Los Angeles to level. Quakes, the *Times* insisted, regularly occurred in Japan, Italy, India, Portugal and Charleston, South Carolina, especially Charleston. These were all good places to stay out of. But do come to Los Angeles.

In 1925, another quake hit Southern California, around Santa Barbara. Again, there was nothing in that to indicate that Los Angeles was in for one of its own: "That Southern California is not readily subject to serious earth disturbances is shown by the fact that the Santa Barbara disaster is the first shake with a death toll . . . in 113 years." Earthquakes, the *Daily News* reported, were "worse in the East than in [the] Southland."

On the afternoon of March 10, 1933, a sizable quake hit the Long Beach area. More than fifty died; masonry buildings, common in the area, collapsed; property damage was in the millions; and for the first time in the history of the Los Angeles Fire Department every piece of equipment it possessed was in the field, working.

The quake began with a roar which created a panic and many of the deaths were attributable to overexcitement. Office workers, believing their buildings were about to collapse, jumped into the streets, adding to the injury toll. Peculiar things happened. A huge flare was seen on the city's north side, the result of a massive electrical short-circuit it was theorized. And the paint peeled off in sheets from the facade of the Hall of Justice.

In the wake of the 1933 quake, nobody poo-pooed future threat, but neither was much positive action taken. To do so would be to risk unfavorable publicity and Los Angeles would never be guilty of that. In 1920, engineer Mulholland was asked what sort of protective measures could be taken in the unlikely possibility of a future quake. "None," he replied, "except saying your prayers."

This it must be admitted is a formidable list of negatives. Enough to sink many a community, but not Los Angeles. Why? Nobody said it better than Mr. J. A. Taylor of Gardena who, in 1924,

had had it up to here with the knockers, and so addressed the following missive to the *Los Angeles Times*:

"Dear Editor: Yes By Hokey dam why do they knock Southern California. Ill tell ye. Theyre Jealous. I come out here in 1912 and Dad burn my leathers. Ill be here in 2012. Git that you Eastern clamity howlers and cronic nockers. When I hear a poor prune knockin some place I jist nachcally put Him down as a Failure . . . Listen you, shut up and listen to me. In the fust place wana impress (heavy on th press) on your delapeidated minds that I was once an Easterner . . . I hung my hat up in Southern California in 1912, and its stills a hangin cause I dont need it. Come out you, as I sed befor, clamity howelers and you can see my hat still hangin because we have reel onest to God weather out here. I have been here Every blessed day and if there was thouands died of the Bubonic plague I did not know it . . . and the Hoof and Mouth disease didn't bother me anymore than the one in Houston . . . But some little frivolous thing happens in California you git out your tin horns and I hope some of you blow your heads off . . . Of course when you peruse this you will put me down as some poor prune That dont know nuthin But listen aforementioned nockers I am wise enuf to pick out the best spot on Gods Green earth to spend my days."

Left. The Long Beach earthquake of 1933 struck late on the afternoon of March 10. Had it hit earlier, when children were in school, the death toll would have been much worse. Masonry and brick construction were common in Southern California because half the population thought earthquakes were a myth and the other half believed in them but didn't think one would ever happen here. Both were wrong.

When oil was struck, the oil usually struck back and, owing to the primitive drilling technology, the resulting gusher might go for days until it was controlled and capped. Meanwhile, the oil pooled on the ground making everybody's life a little stickier.

3

FOLKS, HAVE YOU GOT YOUR TICKET?—OIL

You could hear the money as it gushed out of the ground, you could smell it miles away and, on Sundays, you could load the kids into the family flivver and drive out to visit it. When Los Angeles became Oildorado in the early '20s, they struck not just some oil but an ocean of it. It was one of the largest discoveries ever and the largest so close to a major city. There was the golden sun and the citrus orchards and the hoards of tourists and the real estate boom — and there was more oil than anyone knew what to do with.

It was as funny as it was surprising. In the last century, junketing Eastern businessmen had turned up their noses at Los Angeles. It was inconceivable to them that a city so lacking in readily accessible supplies of energy had any sort of future whatsoever. It was true there were no local forests to burn, no rivers worth damming, no coal to mine, but about oil they should have known better. It was plainly visible at spots where it spontaneously bubbled up out of the ground and congealed with the air to form what the natives called brea, or tar. The only use to which it was put was greasing axles and roofing adobe houses.

E. L. Doheny was no petroleum expert. He was a miner and a total innocent about oil. When he decided to go looking for crude, the tools he used were a pick and shovel. That combination produced only frustration so he turned to using a sharpened tree trunk as a drill. With that he brought in a gusher.

His discovery of an oil field in 1892 transformed a quiet neighborhood near the city's center into a madhouse of exploration. Gingerbread houses and neatly plotted gardens were reduced overnight to scrap lumber and mud. After all the excitement had died down, around the turn of the century, a great many Angelenos had made respectable fortunes, none more so than Doheny who stood at the helm of one of the city's richest families.

No solid new success was counted until 1920, when Standard Oil brought in a well at Huntington Beach. Los Angeles really took note when Bolsa Chica No. 1 blew in with a roar audible fifty miles away. Its initial output, the flush production as it was known in the oil business, was 2,000 barrels a day, sufficient to excite the imp of oil mania and rekindle dreams of sudden wealth in many minds.

Attention focused on a series of raised geological features which were spaced northward from Huntington Beach, one of which was Signal Hill, outside Long Beach. It had got its name eighty years earlier when the crest of the hill was used as a station from which to transmit messages to ships lying off the port of Los Angeles.

There was a problem with Signal Hill. Before the First World War, it had been subdivided, not successfully but enough so that there was a number of householders in residence on the hill. Some of the oil companies, Standard among them, had policies against drilling in residential neighborhoods. Developing an oil field was a massive and hellish undertaking and the fewer public sensitivities it was necessary to trample upon in the process the better. Royal Dutch Shell knew no such reticence and proceeded to lease acreage and drill a test well. On June 21, 1921, Alamitos No. 1 blew in. No one in the area needed to be told what had happened. A rain of oil besotted lawns and coated parked cars, formed in rivulets and coursed through the streets, as the well spewed out mud and oil in its initial and unstoppable regurgitation. Four days later, when the well was capped at 4:00 a.m., a crowd of 500 jubilant spectators was on hand. Alamitos No. 1 settled into a flush production of 1,000 barrels a day, with oil then selling for about $1.20 a barrel.

Signal Hill's life as an unremarkable suburban community abruptly came to an end. A frenzied hoard at once set upon the hill. With it came "roughnecks" ready to drill, experts surveying the next best sites, businessmen scooping up leases with one hand and forming and unforming companies with the other, and rapacious con men and hucksters hungry for the crumbs which inevitably in the confusion eluded other hands. The entire mixture was spiced with an endless stream of gawkers who had heard of the black Old Faithful and come, but who had never in their wildest dreams conceived of anything so financially awe inspiring, so profitably inspirational as this sight of nature belching out its hidden treasures.

The science of oil exploration was then still in its adolescence and, at times, the wisdom it offered wasn't much richer than what the public imagination held: that where there was some oil, there was likely to be more oil and not too far away. The discovery on Signal Hill ignited a boom to the south in the staid community of Long Beach. Before the arrival of black oil, Long Beach had been chiefly noted as the terminus of the Pacific Electric running south from downtown: a community with a pier, a roller coaster and a high proportion of retired Midwestern farmers. Suddenly the streets were filled with people, not Saturday shoppers, regulars, their wicker shopping baskets cradled in the bend of an elbow, but slick newcomers plotting either to slice themselves in on the underground wealth or to sell the local yokels some puny paper representation that seemingly guaranteed entrance on the ground floor.

There *was* oil under Long Beach. For a long time it was seriously debated if a number of recently constructed public buildings shouldn't be torn down to afford the municipality better drilling sites. Ultimately it was decided this wouldn't be necessary; that the wells could exist in close proximity to the buildings and the city still profit. This produced the kind of street scene that, printed on a postcard, became the icon of the new Southern Californian religion of wealth — the office building, the cottage, the bungalow court with a derrick in the front yard. Long Beach became a "taxless city," its royalties in excess of $500,000 a year during the early life of the field.

North of Signal Hill lay the placid farming community of Santa Fe Springs. In the middle of the previous century, a certain Dr. Fulton had tried to capitalize on the sulphur found in the area's springs by founding a health resort. The area's first name was Fulton Springs. The enterprise hadn't prospered and, eventually, the Santa Fe Railroad had become the largest local landlord, dictating a change of name.

In 1920, Santa Fe Springs was populated by families who all knew one another. Their days were devoted to tending crops: apples, oranges, walnuts, corn, beans and tomatoes. One Japanese family grew sugar beets. Pastures were marked by willow fences which had been in place long enough to mature into shade trees. It was so quiet at night that you could hear the bell announcing the shift change at the Maier Brewery fifteen miles away in downtown Los Angeles. A visit to town mean going down to Four Corners, the intersection of Telegraph Road and Northwalk Boulevard, where there was a post office, drug store, grocery and a Methodist Church.

One local farmer was Alphonzo Bell. A relative of one of Los Angeles' pioneer families, he had inherited land in the area and then made purchases until he was farming about 200 acres. Bell, like his neighbors, had trouble getting enough water. Everybody dug wells but not all struck water. Bell was pleased he had. And there was something else. He swore that while digging he had smelled gas and where there was gas, there might be oil. He began pestering the oil companies to drill a test well.

It didn't cost Bell anything to badger the oil companies to lease and drill but each dry hole or "duster" cost $100,000. Union had dug several tests locally over ten years and had little to show for it, so his pleas fell on deaf ears. Standard, however, was eventually persuaded to try its luck. On October 6, 1919, work began on what was called Bell No. 1.

It must have quickened pulses around the well when Alamitos No. 1 came in, and so close. It certainly must have caused Bell himself to take a quick breath and cross his fingers because, the story goes, as the drill bit ground downward, Bell himself was sliding into bankruptcy. His farm was mortgaged and the mortgage was due. Bell was obliged to apply for credit at the local general store.

On the night of October 30, 1919, that changed. Drilling had temporarily stopped at 3,763 feet to allow for maintenance. When it resumed, almost immediately mud and gas cascaded up the shaft. Bell was awakened at once. He was up in time to witness the towering fountain of crude petroleum which announced the discovery of the Santa Fe Springs field.

Within hours the stampede was on. The promoters were still pacing off their leases and firming their deals when the special trains loaded with the best lumber started to arrive. Construction crews went to work immediately cutting the lumber by hand and lifting the heavy beams into place without power machinery. A derrick could be nailed together in three days and now they sprang up like wildflowers, giving the flat plains of southern Los Angeles county a sudden skyline. Derrickmen, drillers and roughnecks — the crews which muscled the heavy drilling machinery to its target — began pouring in from the last discovered field, looking to collect the $7.50 a day some jobs paid. Many brought their families and everything they owned, including their animals, strapped to the sides of ancient Model T's. Home was wherever along the roadside they found a place to stop.

It might not look it but an oil field is a delicate balance of forces which has to be respected if the maximum amount of oil is to be extracted with the minimum expense and effort. But now, respect was out the window. Drilling rights were cut into a thousand pieces and would continue to be splintered for years. It usually took about five months to get down to where the oil was, but that time could be cut in half if the crews worked around the clock. They did, because they were in the race. The general belief was that there was one big pool of oil underground, and the quicker you got there and started sucking it out, the sooner you got rich and the richer you got. If you had two wells then obviously you had twice the sucking power. In fact, one well per four or five acres was all it took to economically drain any underlying oil, but nobody paid any attention to that kind of thinking. Derricks at Santa Fe Springs were planted on an average of one to .73 of an acre, so close together you could walk from one edge of the field to the other on the rough planks of the derrick floors, never once touching the ground.

When a gusher blew in, it would frequently

Getty No. 17 set a record for burning out of control longer than any other well in the Santa Fe field.

be ignited by a spark. An explosion resulted. All the fire crews could do was try and contain the flames while special daredevil firefighters were called in. Dressed in asbestos suits, their strategy was to try and gingerly push a crate of dynamite close enough so that, when it was ignited, the explosion would snuff the flame. Sometimes it worked and sometimes it didn't. In 1928, the most spectacular well fire of all took place when Getty No. 17 came in at Santa Fe Springs and almost immediately exploded. GAS BLOWOUT LOOSES DEMON, the *Times* reported of the blast which lifted up the derrick and threw it a hundred yards. A large crater was dug out and, unrestrained, the oil and gas were ignited. Several derricks nearby were incinerated and seven others were hastily pulled down to prevent their catching fire. Telephone lines nearby were put out of commission and six autos parked a hundred yards away were destroyed. The fire was so intense at first that nobody could get closer than 1,000 feet, and it was impossible to do anything from that distance. The solution was to tunnel underground and, working protected from the heat, stifle the flow. It took more than a month

and a half to extinguish the fire. Getty No. 17 had set a record.

If the fields looked like hell, the boom towns which sprung up on their edges were pure carnival. Tent cities catered to the demands of workers for amusement and hard liquor and the quicker the better. Casinos and gambling dives operated with no respect for the law. Blanket men were common: gamblers with a scrap of cloth, a pair of dice and a bank roll. Prostitutes of every description flocked to where the action was and Santa Fe Springs' new amusement zone went by names like Springs Slums and Gum Grove. The young ladies and those who were neither young nor ladies, worked from tents. They'd wait in front ironing a shirt and they'd iron that same shirt until a client came along.

Prohibition was on but you would never have known it. The bootlegger was an indispensable part of life. The law wasn't much of a problem partly because of Santa Fe Springs' remote location and partly because, without alcohol, tempers would have been shorter than they were. As it was, it was not advisable to visit a bar at night without the company of one or two buddies and perhaps a hunk of metal shaped to fit the hand and kept close by in case of emergency.

The men who worked the fields worked hard and played hard. Times were good, they had steady jobs, and who knew what was next. When they weren't working and were out entertaining themselves or being entertained, they gathered in places like the Four Corners Cafe. There they called the cook Mom and the waitress Aunt Helen and, while the place wasn't much to look at, it was clean and a meal of everything from soup to pie cost no more than 40 cents.

One notable local resident who was not seen around the Four Corners Cafe was the man who had started it all, Alphonzo E. Bell. "I feel," Mr. Bell was frequently quoted as saying, "oil belongs to no one individual." This didn't stop him from accepting the royalties on the oil discovered under his land. He owned close to 200 acres in the middle of one of the richest oil fields in the world which brought him royalties of between $20,000 and $100,000 a month.

Bell remained in Santa Fe Springs immediately after the big strike but, in 1922, a gusher came in, caught fire, and burned telephone poles within a few hundred feet of his home. He decided to move. He packed his family into their "little red roadster" and headed for the Beverly Hills Hotel. Shortly thereafter, he purchased the old Danziger estate, close to 2,000 acres of choice undeveloped land west of Beverly Hills and north of Westwood, which he subdivided and sold under a name his wife dreamed up: Bel-Air. It was described in promotional brochures as "a picturesque domain of homes," and was a huge, secluded estate catering to the well-to-do. "Like the painting of an artist, it is the dream of one man — Alphonzo E. Bell . . .Bel-Air is different." Certainly different from Santa Fe Springs.

Dangerous oil wells and busy red light districts weren't all Bell left behind when he departed the Springs. There had been threats of a kidnapping that were laid to his newly found notoriety. Kidnapping was one way to make money from the fields. Only one way among many.

Another was to own a bit of unremarkable farm land which one morning proves to be sodden with black gold. "Billions from the boneyards of the past," Automobile Club's popular magazine *Touring Topics* called it. "The reader naturally jumps to the conclusion," a writer explained, "that the oil companies get all of the money derived from oil." Nothing could be further from the truth a hungry public was assured. The companies "have to buy or lease the lands upon which to drill . . . and in either case the property owner is greatly benefited."

Greatly benefited? Dipped in cash was more like it. The day before Alamitos No. 1 came in, one house on Signal Hill was for sale for $15,000. The day after, the land alone was offered for $150,000. C. C. Chapman of Fullerton "after years of struggle against the vicissitudes of farm life" found himself on Easy Street. Actually he *owned* Easy Street since the discovery of oil gifted him with more than $3,000,000. With that, he got into his car and drove to downtown L.A. and

the Los Angeles Investment Company which he invested in by buying the building where it was located, which was renamed the C. C. Chapman Building. It didn't take long before tales of sudden wealth had become part of Los Angeles mythology, and everybody knew somebody who had been tapped on the shoulder by the angel of finance.

Not everyone was fortunate enough to own a farm under which oil was about to be discovered. But everybody surely wanted in on the deal and, from the size of the discoveries, it sure seemed like there was more than enough to go around. What the public never realized was that, however many millions or billions were made from selling oil, a thousand times more was made selling the famished public a share. A share of what? A share of the dream.

A share of a producing well even if it wasn't producing much or, better, a share in one that hadn't produced anything but which might. A share of a company that owned nothing but which had the potential to own something. A share in some land which looked hopeless on top but who knew what was under the surface? There was room on the bandwagon for everybody and there would be room just as long as the printing presses were able to churn out the paper certificates which were an indispensable part of the process.

"What impressed me," remembered a tourist to Santa Fe Springs, "was the carnival midway they had there. You have never seen anything like it. It was just like a circus. They had big marquees with signs all over the place. There were gushers of oil spurting out, free lunches, men dressed in cutaway coats that would tell you: 'Invest a dollar and make a fortune.' There was this old man who looked like a retired Baptist preacher: he had a cutaway and a tall brim hat. He made a big talk about this gusher that they were going to drill and bring in: 'On this glorious first day of the year we should bow our heads and thank the Great Lord for this opportunity we have. Amen.' They were selling units. I didn't know what a unit was — I still don't. But we bought some. I wish I still had one. It was a

C.C. Julian, ca 1929. Would you buy a share in an oil well from this man? A lot of people did.

beautiful thing with gushers on it. Then these characters sold out and left town. We were left with no wells and no money."

Los Angeles was, at the moment oil was discovered, chock full of Pas and Mas. "Pa and Ma have come from Iowa," reported a journalist, "leaving the boys to run the farm. They like it in Los Angeles or Long Beach. Pa has a little garden but not much else to occupy him." And Pa and Ma have surplus money.

The schemes — er, the investment propositions — for separating Pa and Ma from their money were many and as ingenious as the human brain in search of easy money can be. The oil lot ruse was typical. A syndicate of promoters bought up ten or twenty acres with some real claim to oil potential. They cut the land up into lots, some as small as 25×50 feet. The buying public got what was, or wasn't, under their lot. The problem was that prime oil land was going for $5,000 an acre. The fees the public was paying for their 25×50 feet added up to a price per acre of $15,000 or more. At that price, there would have to be one hell of a lot of oil underground to make it worth anyone's effort to go in and get it.

When it came to the marketing of investment opportunities of one syllable, there was only one master, one genius whose consummate understanding of his times and of the appetites of his fellow creatures allowed him to forge an empire. The decade of the 1920s posed challenges in many areas, not the least of which was that of confidence schemes. If, as writer Upton Sinclair observed, the oil game was like heaven where many are called and few are chosen, Chauncey C. Julian — C. C. to one and all and his was a household name — was the man chosen.

There was little distinguished in C. C. Julian's early years, nothing to presage his eventual rise to fame. He was born in Winnipeg, Canada, the son of a failed gentleman farmer. He attended a business college and later dabbled in real estate where he made substantial sums only to lose them in sudden business downswings. As a young man, he traveled to California where he worked in the oil industry around Bakersfield.

In 1918, Julian drifted to Texas, lured by the big oil strikes. While there, he heard of the activity at Huntington Beach. He raced to California, and somehow put together $140,000 with which to drill a well. It was a total bust.

In 1922, C. C. managed to get a small leasehold in Santa Fe Springs for $30,000, borrowed, of course. The terms of the lease required C. C. to spud in (begin drilling a well) within thirty days, and, to do that, he had to somehow raise an additional $100,000.

Let's assume that, until 1922 and the Springs, C.C. was an honest man. Maybe it was the sight of so much money being made by so many other people that drove him mad. If not mad, perhaps the turmoil in that financial furnace distorted his character, forced him into a moral corner, compelled him to accept a less than strict interpretation of the laws. Let us say this so that what follows is in some sense understandable. For facing disaster, mortgaged to the hilt, C.C. Julian somehow reached down inside himself and found talents he didn't know he possessed, talents which marked him as one of the great public relations geniuses of his age.

C.C. JULIAN BREAKS INTO SANTA FE SPRINGS — THE GUSHER OIL FIELD OF AMERICA, read the cheery headlines on ads C.C. inserted into the city's newspapers. There was nothing new about oil advertising. Ads were as extravagant and promised as much as they could get away with and still be accepted for placement on the financial pages. C.C.'s ads used no slick graphics, just columns of type. The words weren't fancy, anything but. You couldn't put your finger on it but there was something special about C.C. in print. Something that came across as plain talk from a straight shooter, with a touch of good old-fashioned evangelical fervor. C.C. was somebody you'd invite into your kitchen and pour a mug of coffee for while you discussed politics and finances. C.C. was a guy you could trust, a guy who'd put his arm around your shoulder and, in words of one syllable, lay out an uncomplicated investment opportunity, a sure fire way of getting rich quick.

C.C. Julian didn't place ads, he waged campaigns which, splashed across the heretofore proper, even recondite financial pages of Los Angeles newspapers, stood the money barons on their ear. Every day there was something new in what C.C. had to say, something calculated to bring the investing temper of Mr. Joe Angeleno to fever pitch. These ads climaxed Julian's first campaign, in July, 1922. It was a big success so he did the only thing he could—started another.

"I want you with me and I am going to make you the cleanest offer ever tended the public in this or any other oil field," C.C. announced. C.C. was no city slicker, he swore he had "no board of directors at fat salaries to juggle your profits," and he wasn't going to mislead people and tell them that "I drilled the Lakeview Gusher at Maricopa or the Big Trapshooter in Louisiana." Oil, C.C. admitted, was a gamble and he had "shot his bank roll when I bought this tract," but here's what he was going to do. For every $100 you sent him, he would pay you 1/1,750th part of all profits realized. "Just mail your check to me for the amount you want to shoot or come in and see me personally." And when C.C. struck oil he'd forward your profits. That was simple wasn't it? If the well was fully subscribed, C.C. would make $175,000.

C.C's advertising bandwagon was off. Each day there was a new ad, with the distinctive bold headlines followed by reams of folksy chatter: "NO STOCKS! NO UNITS! ACTION IS MY SLOGAN . . . SANTA FE SPRINGS NEVER BEFORE PERHAPS NEVER AGAIN . . . HOLD HER DEACON, ACTION, ACTION, ACTION . . . DO YOU REALIZE THAT MY OFFER IS NOTHING SHORT OF THE 'OLD CAT'S TONSILS'? Julian refuses to accept your money unless you can afford to lose! Widows and orphans, this is no investment for you! . . . Every $100 you put in should pay you back $3,000 . . . Do you realize that I am offering you the squarest and surest opportunity ever submitted to you and it is not going to last forever? If you were given a tip on a race horse that was a strong favorite at odds of thirty to one, would you place $50 or $100 on him to win? I am that race horse . . . and take it from me I am going to win!"

Day after day the ads appeared. Money flooded in. It came in the mail, it was delivered in person, and, when he counted it, there was $220,000—considerably more than he'd set out to raise. Now C.C. knew his destiny.

With his first ad campaign not yet completed, C.C. suddenly announced: "Keep your hand on your bankroll, folks. I have another sweet deal brewing at SANTA FE SPRINGS on the most won-derful piece of oil land that you have ever laid your hands on. The outfit that owns it are sure 'hard-boiled' but if I get it it's the 'Eagle's Hips' and you will be in on the ground floor and I guarantee there will be no basement."

C.C. wasn't exactly telling the truth. There were no mysterious negotiations underway. He was planning to drill his second well on his original leasehold, but putting it the way he did gave it more life. C.C.'s second syndicate raised another $220,000. C.C. followed with a third, a fourth and a fifth. In six months, working from the comfort and safety of his downtown office through the business pages of the daily newspapers, C. C Julian had catapulted himself into the public eye and lifted over $688,000 out of the public pocket.

Julian was, of course, actually drilling wells at Santa Fe Springs. And a very strange thing happened. His first well came in and started paying out profits. Never mind that the profits were nowhere near what C.C. had prophesied or that none of C.C.'s other wells would hit pay dirt. In the public consciousness, his reputation was made, his stature was unassailable. C.C. was a hero of the little guy.

What the public didn't know was that C.C. was juggling the books with the aplomb of a circus seal. He had been broke in 1922 when it had all begun. By the end of 1923, he had a bank account in six figures. The high six figures.

In mid-1923, C. C. Julian crossed the Rubicon that separated mere financial manipulation from inspired fraud. C.C. announced, in his ads, that he intended founding his own Julian Petroleum Corporation, which immediately and affectionately became known as Julian Pete. Julian Pete would be one big oil company, complete with its own wells, pipelines, tank farms, refineries and gas stations. Pete would be the little guy's major oil company. The money would be raised from C.C.'s devoted admirers.

California's corporations commission did not approve of C.C. or the manner in which he was operating. C.C. alleged it was part of a conspiracy, emanating from downtown Los Angeles, de-

They trucked them in on sucker buses, the eager, the willing, and those some shade in between. First they were given lunch and then afforded the opportunity, for a small investment, to make a fortune.

voted to doing in the Julian dream. So C.C. picked up his corporation, at least on paper, and carried it to Nevada where the laws were not so strict. C.C. then returned to L.A. and, thumbing his nose at the state, began selling stock in Pete, the sales aided by the publicity C.C. was getting from his running battle with the powers that be.

One thing the powers could do was sic the cops on C.C. In December of 1923, responding to pressure from the publisher of the *Times*, Harry Chandler, the FBI assigned an agent/accountant to study C.C.'s books. At first C.C. cooperated but, after a few months, he balked. The FBI man had no alternative but to suspend his inquiry and submit a partial report. He found no evidence of wrongdoing.

The early '20s were a time when it was very much anything goes on the stock market, and practices which today would be good for ten years as a guest of the Federal government were common and created little talk. Even so, C.C.'s manipulations alarmed the downtown types. C.C. had sold out the first Pete stock issue in just fifty-five days, oversubscribing it by nearly $2 million. When it came time to produce the receipts for the oversubscription, C.C. said they

had been destroyed in a fire which some doubting Thomases found convenient. Matters reached boiling point in February of 1924 when continued public speculation, rumors and official attacks all merged, and Pete was facing a panic. STOP JULIAN PANIC TALK! SAVE 43,000 INVESTORS! roared the *Daily News*, declaiming the crisis of confidence which could destroy the corporation.

A blue-ribbon committee, representing the cream of the established financial community, was appointed to inspect C.C.'s operations and pass judgment. They were loaded into a fleet of expensive cars and, headed by C.C. in his Pierce-Arrow limo, set off on a tour of the Julian empire. At Whittier, C.C. pointed out what he said were some of his leases. At Santa Fe Springs, it was his now famous wells one, two and three. They weren't quite pumping the 4,000 barrels a day C.C. had said they were. More like 400. There were pipelines, tank farms and, at Wilmington, oil-loading facilities followed by a box lunch. "Help yourselves," C.C. told his judges, "there's plenty."

A few weeks later, the committee rendered its Olympian judgment. Pete was okay. C.C. had won another round.

Certain of C.C.'s enemies weren't satisfied when the FBI's accountant had returned with no evidence of Julian wrongdoing. Pressure was again brought to bear on FBI Director J. Edgar Hoover. In late 1924, a second FBI agent/accountant was assigned to Julian. In November, a second report was submitted to the Bureau.

This one had a curious feature to it, an extended interview with Julian in which he eloquently put forth his view of events, delineating what he was convinced was a conspiracy against him. What made this interview doubly interesting was the fact that it had been submitted to Julian before it was handed over to the FBI. And the agent, when questioned about when a fuller report could be expected, replied that the company's affairs were complicated and such an audit would require the better part of a year.

Warning bells must have sounded at FBI headquarters because, in early 1925, a third agent/accountant was assigned to the case. The assignment of this latest agent might have been hastened by the fact that agent number two, when recalled to Washington, had resigned from Federal service and taken a job with Julian Pete.

What agent number three learned wasn't curious, it was downright peculiar. For example, while agent number two was supposedly investigating Pete on behalf of the FBI, he was also preparing financial documents for Pete's Accounting Department, documents which C.C. was using to buttress his case.

Then there was the matter of the audit the blue-ribbon investigating committee had had prepared and upon which it had based its judgment. It had been ordered form the prestigious accounting firm of Price Waterhouse. The audit showed Pete with a cash surplus. Yet the FBI's accountant was able to ascertain that, immediately before the audit, Pete had been reporting a deficit. Numerous other accounting oddities turned up, especially deals which in one light looked great for Pete but which, viewed in their fuller context, were actually big losses. The final straw was that the man who had done the report had been paid an exceptionally handsome sum of

Right. When the oil boom began, everybody wanted in and there were those promoters only too willing to let the public in—for a price. The idea was to get a share: a share in a well, a lot, a house, a lot with a well, a well with a house—it didn't matter. Just get a share.

ORANGES AND OIL

COPYRIGHT 1922 BY HOMI C. BAILEY.

Why are we wearing this satisfied smile?
Because we've "MADE GOOD" through our faith and our toil.
We live and, let live in a land that's worth while,
And share with our neighbors our "Oranges and Oil."

THIS MATINEE TRIP
MAKES A BIG HIT

Our Saturday Afternoon Trip has proved such a splendid success, and we have decided to extend the courtesy to
MONDAY, WEDNESDAY, SATURDAY
2:00 P. M. Sharp
Ample accommodations have been provided to take care of all who wish to go as our guests.
Enjoy the cool ocean breeze and the mountain scenery!

See the Beauties of Southern California
Study Intimately the State's Two Chief Products

money for the amount of work involved.

Once again, the deft hand of C.C., the accomplished charmer and juggler, was sensed. "I cannot help feeling," the FBI's third and final agent reported, "that [the Price Waterhouse accountant] is preparing the most favorable statement he can possibly prepare . . . and when considering the possible defendants in this case I think [his] part in this conspiracy should be weighed carefully."

All of this was happening backstage. Publicly, Pete, despite its bill of health from the blue-ribbon group, was still encountering unending difficulties. But C.C. was a master of the unexpected and now he performed his greatest trick. Insisting that it was personal animosity alone that was affecting Pete, C.C. announced he was stepping aside, leaving the company that bore his name, practically giving it away in the hopes that new management could save the company from being a political football.

C.C. seemingly found the perfect replacement. S. C. Lewis was everything C. C. Julian wasn't. Measured where Julian was flamboyant, nondescript where C.C. was stylish, Lewis was the kind of man people naturally seemed to call "judge." After C.C. withdrew, Lewis met with and received a kind of formal laying on of hands from J. F. Sartori, the powerful head of Security Bank. Sartori pronounced himself pleased with Julian's replacement. So pleased he consented to loan Pete money.

There were a few angles to Lewis that a fuller investigation might have turned up. For instance, when Lewis came to Los Angeles to conclude his deal with C.C., he had had trouble paying his hotel bill. Or the fact that Lewis' old company, Lewis Petroleum, was being investigated for mail fraud violations. Lewis was apparently fond of telling stockholders and potential investors things like this company owned gas stations which it in fact didn't. Questions might have been raised had not downtown been so delighted to be rid of C. C. Julian.

The biggest question of all would have been that of Lewis' close relationship with Jacob Ber-

man. Berman had a few strange habits. For instance, conducting business under a series of aliases. In fact, had Los Angeles asked about Jack Bennett, the name under which Berman was known in town, it would have been found that he was the notorious operator of "bucket shops," fraudulent stock con games.

What no one appreciated at first was that Lewis and Berman, with a few adroit strokes of the accountant's quill, had succeeded in buying Julian Pete with money borrowed from the company itself. Since the company was behind the eight ball, the loan from Sartori had helped considerably. But more money was needed, according to Lewis, if Pete was to expand. He should have said, if the company was just to stay afloat.

To get the money they wanted, Lewis and Berman embraced the stock market and its mechanisms in a way C.C. hardly dared dream about. They proceeded to manipulate Julian Pete shares using a stock brokerage house they purchased, and relying upon the considerable public good will remaining toward C.C., and the widespread fascination in the stock as a way of making money.

Lewis and Berman formed pools to force the price of Pete to fluctuate up and down and thereby profit. For the money to run these pools, they paid exorbitant rates of interest. When the loans became due, they rolled them over at even higher interest rates. A lot of that interest was paid in shares of Pete stock.

That something was very wrong should have been obvious to all. In October of 1925, 245,000 shares of Pete stock were traded on the Los Angeles Exchange. Not so great a number perhaps, except that it was 15,000 more shares than Pete was legally allowed to have outstanding. That was just the beginning. In the first few months of 1926, figures indicated that every single share of Julian Pete was being traded on the average four times a month!

Lewis and Berman, simply, were watering Julian Pete stock. Somewhere a printing press was merrily chattering away, turning out countless numbers of Julian Pete stock certificates which were cheerfully handed out by Lewis in exchange for money. Lewis and Berman were operating a private mint and, for the moment, no one was the wiser.

C.C. himself had disappeared although, when he left Pete, something of the magic went out of him. Early in 1926, C.C. was back on the financial pages with a new scheme. "Death Valley and 'Her Hidden Treasures' — 'That's My Baby Now' " C.C. proclaimed. He had a new company, Western Lead Mines and Western Lead, according to C.C., owned a hundred-million-dollar silver-lead mine. On January 30, 1926, to considerable public and insider interest, trading in Western Lead opened on the Los Angeles Exchange at $1.50 a share. It closed up.

"HERE'S A HOT ONE . . . WHAT? NO SPINACH??? Not so you'd notice, nor bananas either, but, oh boy, oodles of SILVER-LEAD," read the ads. C.C. was up to his old tricks. By March, Western Lead had risen to over $3.00 a share. It was then a series of bear raids hit the stock. In one day it dropped seventy points. Crowds of anxious speculators big and little, bloodhounds who smelled the impending massacre, jammed into the downtown stock exchange building to witness the frenzied trading at first hand. Police had to be called to handle the crowds. With the stock poised at ninety cents a share, the bears could be sensed. But then, mirabile dictu! C.C's office issued a statement that a massive new vein of lead had been uncovered and the hand of the bears was stayed. What would have made a dreadful soap opera was being played out for real on Spring Street and in the newspapers eagerly scooped up by every literate Angeleno. Would C.C. survive the onslaughts of his enemies another day? All Los Angeles wanted to know.

C.C. calmly stared down his antagonists. He called reporters into his office, showed them two rocks streaked with lead and silver which he said came from his properties, and insisted the bottom line was that "Western Lead is worth millions or it isn't worth a cent." Hard to argue with. "It's a speculation," C.C. admitted, "but the best I

know of." For the moment Los Angeles agreed.

Before long, C.C. felt confident enough to mount an excursion to his properties. A special train was chartered: twelve pullmans and two diners to carry C.C. and 340 guests to Death Valley. At the Tonopah and Tidewater station, closest to the mine site, a fleet of autos gathered up the junketeers and conveyed them past Beatty and Rhyolite and Bullfrog, through narrow Titus Canyon to Leadville. It was the greatest moment in Leadville history.

A banquet was offered at Ole's Inn and 1,120 were served a hearty dinner, accompanied by a jazz band from Los Angeles. The Lieutenant Governor of Nevada welcomed C.C. It was all swell and the boom was on. By August, Leadville had grown large enough to merit its own post office.

Back in L.A., the waters had not calmed for C.C. His old antagonist, the state corporations' commissioner, dragged him into a hearing. C.C. was more than equal to the task and, to the delight of Los Angeles, the hearings became known as the "C. C. Julian Circus," during which C.C. "stepped into the sawdust ring and [took] the whip away from the commission which would make him dance to its music."

One interesting fact did emerge, and it concerned the manner in which Western Lead stock had made it to the L.A. Exchange. Prior to listing, officers of the Exchange, including the president, had been given the opportunity to buy shares at one-third the opening price of $1.50. Since the stock had immediately doubled, they made a handsome profit. The Exchange president insisted there was nothing irregular about the transaction.

As the summer wore on, there was bad news from Leadville. The claims made for the mine weren't panning out. C.C. insisted he was as surprised as anyone. Trading in Western Lead was suspended.

C.C.'s roller coaster made S. C. Lewis and Jake Berman acutely uncomfortable. If there was no formal relationship, their company still bore the Julian name. So Lewis decided to do something about it. He decided to create an even larger company by merging Julian Pete with some smaller companies he'd acquired to form what he called California Eastern.

Lewis had convinced the cream of L.A.'s financial society to support him, men such as banker Motley Flint, founder of Flintridge, whose brother was a former U.S. Senator. Through his powerful connections, Lewis had put together $12,000,000 in financing for his new company.

Of course, for appearance' sake, it was best to clear away the few dark clouds that hovered over Julian Pete. There were persistent rumors of a stock overissue. Lewis agreed there might be a slight overissue. If that proved the case, he was more than willing to personally put up the money to buy back the stock. And then there was the widespread knowledge of the pools in Julian stock formed to influence the stock's market price. To deal with these, Flint and other bankers helped Lewis form yet another pool. And to control that pool, another. And so on ad infinitum. Before long, everybody in the know was in one pool or another: Joe Toplitzky, real-estate operator; Louis B. Mayer, head of MGM Studios; Harry Haldeman, head of the near-fanatical Better America Foundation (and grandfather of H. R. Haldeman); Cecil B. de Mille, director. Still the price of Julian stock floundered and so more pools were formed until it reached the point where one pool, the "Tijuana pool," was composed of members of Los Angeles' criminal syndicate and race track touts. All of the pools were glued together by Julian stock.

In liquidating the pools, the usual procedure was simply to sell the shares pool members held. But Lewis knew that, with so much stock out, the effect on the price of Pete stock would be disastrous. So he settled on an alternative plan. If pool members would retain their stock, he would offer them bonus payments in cash. At the moment pool members agreed, something magical happened under California law. The pools ceased being pools and became loans to the company, loans at usurious rates of interest, and the pool

participants looked, de facto, to be conspirators in a plot to commit usury.

On May 5, 1927, the continued rumors of an overissue in Pete stock forced L.A. Exchange officials to act. Trading was suspended. Julian Pete was finished.

The stunning news of the collapse of Julian Pete reverberated in every neighborhood of Los Angeles for weeks, months and years to come. The company had been a delicately balanced pyramid in which 42,000 investors, large and small, had been enmeshed.

The first question was how large had been the overissue. Large enough that its size could never be exactly determined. As far as anyone could made out something like a paper value of $150,000,000 (somewhere close to three-quarters of a billion dollars in today's dollars) had been printed up, sold and resold around Los Angeles. Overnight, $40,000,000 had simply disappeared from the city.

C.C., ironically, had been unscathed by the fall of the company that bore his name. He was, of course, only too delighted to offer any comments the press might desire of him.

The real culprits, or at least the ones nearest at hand, were Lewis and Berman. They and half of Los Angeles' social register were eventually indicted for one or another crime arising from the inflation and deflation of the Julian balloon. The *New York Times* called the indictments a "super-sensation."

In January of 1928, the trials began, Lewis and Berman first. The prosecutor was District Attorney Asa Keyes, the vigorous accuser of Aimee Semple McPherson. But something was wrong. Keyes left the preparation of the state's case to his subordinates. Even the judge was forced to comment on the laggard manner in which the prosecution conducted its case. In May, the jury handed down its decision: not guilty.

It was the most stunning verdict ever uttered in a Los Angeles courtroom. The press and public were shocked. And if the general mood at the time of the failure of Pete stock was for a necktie

The Boy Wonder, former District Attorney Asa Keyes (rhymes with eyes), being led away to San Quentin. Keyes is the second man in the elevator.

party, when the culprits were turned loose, tempers really rose. The *Examiner,* reminding the public the trial had cost $25,000, said the verdict "makes robbery easy in Los Angeles." The *Times* charged the verdict was the result of "the incompetent and bungling manner in which the case was presented." No sooner were Lewis and Berman set free than they were arrested by the Federal government. It was greatly hoped the net of Federal justice would be drawn tauter than had been the case in Los Angeles.

In January, 1929, Los Angeles at last found out what had gone wrong. Incredible new revelations shook the city. They originated in a highly unlikely corner: the Spring Street tailor shop of Ben Getzoff. Milton Pike, a disgruntled assistant, had gone to the police with a fantastic tale. What Getzoff cut in his shop was not fabric but deals, deals which included his friends D.A. Asa Keyes, and Jake Berman. To support his story, Pike offered a pile of papers: notes taken on business cards, scrap paper, anything at hand, which together formed a diary recording dates and the names of individuals involved in the rigging of the Julian Pete prosecution. Berman turned

state's evidence and admitted he had given Keyes, through Getzoff, cash, a chaise lounge, golf clubs, two automobiles and a watch. Keyes was tried and sent to San Quentin.

Lewis and Berman eventually did time in Federal prisons. The rich and powerful were never brought to trial. The *Times* urged L.A. to forget about it all. After all, while vast sums of money had jumped from pocket to pocket in an unsavory manner, the money was still here in Los Angeles. Somewhere.

The man who had started it all with his shrewd manipulation of local sentiment met a curious end. He left Los Angeles after the Julian trials and tried his luck syndicating wells in Oklahoma. And the funny thing is that history repeated itself. His first well struck oil and C. C. Julian was again off and running. This time, however, he made the mistake of conducting much of his campaign through the mails, and the Feds decided he had overstepped the line. A warrant was issued for C.C. One step ahead of the law, he fled the country.

He was next located in the Astor House in Shanghai where he insisted he was "entitled to a better break... than I received in the United States." Whatever it was C.C. was planning came to nothing. Millions of dollars had passed through his hands and now, in early 1934, he was down to his last dollar. He used it to buy a friend a drink. Then he staged a banquet. Midway through the festivities he excused himself, went up to his room, and took poison. He was buried in Shanghai. Nine people attended his funeral.

It is part of the enduring mythology of Los Angeles that, sometime prior to his death, C. C. Julian sat down and wrote an autobiography. And that, in this tome, he unhesitatingly named names, implicating in a conspiracy the rich and powerful of Los Angeles and Washington, in a tale of political corruption which supposedly reached into the White House. The manuscript was said to have survived C.C. Who knows? One day it may actually turn up.

James Edgar Davis, Los Angeles
police chief, who liked a well-cut and
well-pressed uniform.

4

PICKING THE PUBLIC POCKET AND OTHER RELATED FORMS OF EQUALLY PROFITABLE ENTERPRISE

Nobody in Los Angeles didn't like reading about cops and robbers. Fires and floods were good for headlines. But the juicy stories that kept readers addicted to their daily dose of newsprint involved some attempt to steal the public purse, or profit by corrupting the public morals, or better yet, both. And, best of all, if those doing the pilfering or corrupting were police. If Los Angeles loved reading tales of cops and robbers, it was partly because it was often hard to tell them apart.

There were laws here, laws against prostitution, making book, gambling and, during Prohibition, alcohol. Curiously, these laws were occasionally enforced, although not even then were all citizens required to obey them. All this made great reading.

Now wait. This is supposed to be Los Angeles, Dubuque transplanted, with a heightened awareness of and resistance to sin. But, of course, for every Mayor Walker there was a Mayor Thompson and Tammany Hall had nothing on the Pendergast machine. So Los Angeles' resistance to sin was just ordinary. And the city's awareness of it? Why, the day that passed without some reminder was a dull day indeed.

It would be disappointing if Los Angeles did not give this traditional civic set-to its own special flavor. Los Angeles never had a criminal mob. Genteel L.A. had a syndicate. Anything but a gang that couldn't shoot straight, it was a gang that didn't shoot at all if it could be avoided. A real tough-guy racketeer like they had back East would have laughed himself silly over a kingpin whose name was Charles Henry Crawford.

But they did call Charlie Crawford the Grey Wolf, if not for his ferocity then for his cunning. Born in Ohio, Charlie learned the twin arts of criminal organization and political fixing in Seattle. There he operated a casino whose silent partners included the mayor and chief of police. When a reform-minded city council was elected intent on changing this, Charlie hastily departed for Los Angeles.

He opened the Maple Bar at Fifth and Maple and it became known as a watering hole for those interested in the transaction of the public's business. That Charlie converted the former rooming house upstairs and stocked it with young ladies

MAPLE BAR
C.H. CRAWFORD
230 EAST FIFTH STREET
LOS ANGELES CAL.

The interior of Charlie Crawford's Maple Bar, a hideaway for those interested in doing business downtown, and for those from downtown interested in the business.

didn't hurt his popularity a bit. What made Charlie even more popular was that he was a good listener. Maybe because, when he spoke, his Adam's apple bobbed uncontrollably and, owing to an infection, his voice was effeminate. So he listened, learned a lot of secrets and eventually the phrase "see Charlie about it" gained a real currency.

In the bad old days, the fix which protected vice operations was a penny-ante affair. Cops on the beat were paid off, kept their share and passed the rest along until it reached the mayor. The generation which managed this system met its demise in 1921, when a political upstart, George Cryer, defeated the establishment's man, Meredith "Pinky" Snyder, for mayor.

Cryer looked like Woodrow Wilson but had less flash. Behind him, pulling the strings in his administration, was a young lawyer with a talent for politics. Kent Kane Parrot. And, aside from his organizational skills, Parrot had something else that de facto made him an insider: he had been a football star at USC and had attended USC Law School as well. With that record, election to what was long called the "courthouse gang," the old boy connection of USC-trained lawyers who ran downtown, was no problem.

Charlie Crawford was the sort of man Kent Parrot could get along with: a backroom organizer who shunned the limelight. The syndicate Crawford assembled mirrored this. Bookmaking and betting were supervised by Ezekiel "Zeke" Caress, a native of Los Angeles. He was the perfect lieutenant. Totally colorless, he looked like the accountant he was and neither smoked, drank nor chased women. Caress's one moment of public notoriety came in 1931 when he was kidnapped. The affair became a comic opera when no one agreed to pay the ransom demanded. Caress indignantly offered to pay it himself but, of course, he could only do so with a check. His kidnappers were arrested trying to cash his check.

The Gans brothers, Joe and Bob, former wholesale tobacco merchants, ran the slot machines. A profitable line, Bob Gans eventually amassed a fortune estimated at $15–20,000,000.

In charge of casinos and gambling was Guy "Stringbean" McAfee. Formerly a fireman on the Southern Pacific, McAfee had joined the LAPD after, he said, having seen a cop roll a drunk. McAfee was discharged from the force in 1917 for running a crap game in the police assembly room. He was reinstated and assigned to the vice or Purity Squad. Often, before a big raid, McAfee would be noticed whistling into a telephone. When the patrol wagons got to their target, the evidence would be mysteriously gone.

The biggest badman in Crawford's ranks, the one pug ugly who looked like he'd been supplied by Central Casting, was Marco Albori, alias Albert Marco. Another Seattle import, Marco wore pinstriped suits and a permanent sneer. His constant companion was the diminutive Augustus "Chito" Sasso, as taciturn as his boss was outgoing. Marco's exploits were legendary. Once he sat down in a Bunker Hill rooming house and dropped $260,000 playing cards with Nick the Greek. He had a taste for the fast life.

Anywhere else but Los Angeles, Marco would have gone down in a hail of bullets. His actual end was less heroic. One evening in 1928, he was whooping it up on the Ship Cafe, a popular nightspot on the Venice Pier. Marco got a little too friendly with a young lady and, when her husband objected, the two men stepped outside. Marco was getting the worse of it when he pulled a rod and fired, injuring his opponent.

Unfortunately for Marco, the beat cop who was called proved impervious to both his braggadocio and his attempts at bribery. Marco was arrested for assault. It happened that, that night, the captain of the Venice detail was Strongarm Dick Steckel, formerly of Chinatown. He arrived at the Ship much after Marco's arrest but that didn't stop him from letting it be known he was "the man who got Marco," a reputation that helped elevate him to the chief's chair. Marco eventually was sent to San Quentin and, when he'd served his time, he was deported home to Italy.

The Los Angeles Police Department was supposedly combating the Crawford organization. The force was not hampered by professionalism, and the wheels of justice, it was generally conceded, ran throughout the '20s and '30s well greased. When the Cryer administration took over, it did so on a promise to reform the department. Cryer's choice for chief was Charles A. Jones, a low-ranked officer not connected with the thoroughly politicized hierarchy. Jones struggled manfully but, in months, tossed up his hands. "No one can run the Los Angeles Police Department," he said as he departed. "The job is not worth the grief which attends it. No sir, they couldn't give me the job on a silver platter with inlaid gold trimmings."

Next to receive the platter was Colonel W. Everington who had no experience in law enforcement but who had been a war hero. "My only policy is to enforce the law," Everington said stoutly. "I have no debts to pay, no axe to grind, and there are no strings on me. I know nothing about the police department and am not ashamed to admit it."

Everington soon learned that the chief of Los Angeles' police was only supposed to enforce most, not all, laws and apply them to most, not all, citizens. He was furious at the double standard that witnessed downtown businessmen at church on Sunday piously supporting their ministers in lambasting the police for inaction while, the rest of the week, these same businessmen

Above left. Guy McAfee, in training for his future career as head of Los Angeles vice coalition, as a member of the LAPD.

Above right. Marco Albori, alias Albert Marco, who had a reputation as a stylish dresser and a good man with his fists.

Below left. Kent Kane Parrot, USC-trained lawyer, unofficial head of the informal courthouse gang, and the brains behind the administration of Mayor George Cryer.

Below right. Chief of Police Roy "Strongarm Dick" Steckel, a former mill worker, had no reputation for finesse as a cop.

collected handsome rents from the buildings in which vice activities were housed. But having realized this was the way, Everington made the mistake of speaking out against it and, within four months, his position as chief was taken away. "The fact of the matter is," he declared upon involuntarily retiring, "that I haven't run the department since I was appointed chief. An honest man can't do that. A crook can be chief, though, if he's clever enough not to get caught."

Did Mayor Cryer consciously take Everington's words to heart with his next appointment? Who knows. The mayor appointed as chief, detective Louis D. Oakes. Oakes had first come to public notice as one of the officers who had arrested the kidnappers of Mrs. Gladys Witherell. It was a sensational case: a handsome young woman, well-placed in society, abducted for God knows what maniacal reasons by seedy thugs. This sort of thing just didn't happen. When Mrs. Witherell was safely home, Oakes was awarded a gold badge inlaid with diamonds.

As chief, Oakes endeared himself to downtown business interests by his unstinting antipathy to organized labor. It was Oakes who arrested writer Upton Sinclair for trying to read the Constitution to a public meeting. Oakes also arrested the man who succeeded Sinclair but who didn't try and read the Constitution. What *he* did was to comment: "This is a most delightful climate."

Another of Oakes' exploits thrilled the public. The notorious desperado, "Little Phil" Alguin, had murdered a cop and made good his escape across the Mexican border. Oakes followed, accompanied by the beautiful Catherine Uribe who was helping the chief in exchange for the release of her husband, being held in Los Angeles for stealing a Cadillac. The exploits of Oakes and Uribe hardly endeared them to the Mexican government.

But Oakes had real trouble. He just wasn't very good as a departmental politician. And then there was the night Oakes was arrested in his chief's car, a half-empty liquor bottle on the floor and a half-dressed young lady on his lap.

There was another story about how Oakes met his end. He had had as his nemesis from the start the Reverend "Fighting Bob" Shuler. Shuler correctly noticed that no matter how showy the chief's exploits, the fact of the matter was vice was rarely if ever bothered. So Shuler was on Oakes' case. He got a tip and, as a result, said he saw Oakes emerging from a hotel of very poor repute with a young lady on each arm. Oakes' tenure as chief lasted slightly more than a year.

Cryer's next selection as chief was pure genius. Berkeley's August Vollmer was the nation's most famous cop, the man called the father of American police work. No believer in strong arm methods, Vollmer was a political liberal who created the science of policing.

It went without saying he was incorruptible and, since he was beholden to no faction, he was disliked by all. His innovations included the keeping of statistics, the introduction of a "flying squad" to hit problem areas, and the first police academy. But as his year came to an end, his antagonists were only too glad to see him go. His term was up in September and, as that month approached, billboards appeared announcing "The First of September will be the Last of August."

In the mayoral elections of 1925, Cryer and Parrot had outmaneuvered crusty Harry Chandler at the *Times*. Chandler wanted Cryer out. Parrot skillfully put Cryer into every camp that was opposed to the *Times*. Chandler's candidate was Federal judge Benjamin Bledsoe. Parrot made eloquently clear who was backing the judge by posting billboards that read: "Harry calls him Ben." About the same time, readers of the *Daily News* were electing Chandler the unannounced Boss of Los Angeles. A ceremony was held on the steps of City Hall to swear Harry in but he rudely refused to appear.

Cryer's next appointment as chief was designed in part to mollify Chandler. James Edgar Davis was born in Texas and had joined the force in 1912. He'd served on the Purity Squad with McAfee. Davis' aproach to police work was summed up in an anecdote from his early years. He'd shot it out with a hood. Out of ammo, he'd

Fighting Bob Shuler, when he was finally sentenced for contempt of court, said he welcomed prison and the martyrdom it conferred on him. He also had his lawyers fight the conviction all the way to the State Supreme Court and, when that august body refused to free him, Bob was forced to cut a deal with his antagonists. He wanted out, and he got out early.

charged his adversary and slammed his empty revolver down on the miscreant's head hard enough to bend the barrel.

Davis was a great believer in the police although he knew and cared little about the law he was supposed to enforce. He had a recipe for success in his beat days: stop and search everybody he came upon. Later, as chief, he developed this into what he called the "blockade system." Police would close off an intersection and stop and search every car coming through. When citizens objected, the chief would nostalgically recall the good old days when the public knew its place. He bemoaned the "automobile complex," that "the public resents being stopped and looked over even though that stopping and examining is for the protection of the honest and law-abiding section of the community."

"Chief Davis honestly and sincerely believes," reported a newspaper, "that the whole country would be much better off if the whole question of constitutional rights was forgotten and left to the discretion of the police." Davis let it be known that, as far as he was concerned, constitutional rights were of "no benefit to anybody but crooks and criminals."

Fighting Bob Shuler abhorred Davis as much as he had disliked Oakes. "To begin with," the reformer said, "Davis is too 'purty' to be police chief," referring to Davis' well-known predilection for a sharply creased uniform. "I can't get it into my head that a man with a pink complexion who looks like he had a massage every morning and his fingernails manicured, is a good chief of police."

One thing Fighting Bob was never guilty of was a manicure. Born in Virginia, he was educated as a circuit-riding Methodist minister. Posted to Texas, his antiliquor views got him in trouble and he'd been shipped out to Los Angeles and Trinity Methodist South.

Fighting Bob proved a capable fund raiser. In a few years, he'd attracted a healthy congregation and $250,000 in donations. His secret was his affability, his countrified, heart-to-heart style. If others wrung their hands over fine points of

theology, Bob blasted away with sermons like: "The Vernon Country Club versus Democracy: How Long will Los Angeles Stand for It?" Bob was the all-time city gossip, perfectly capable of shooting from the hip at the drop of a rumor, but always promising and delivering lurid revelations to an eager audience.

The revelations poured out in Bob's sermons, in his own magazine which was modestly called *Bob Schuler's Magazine,* and in an endless spate of privately published booklets. But his big boost came when a contributor gifted him with $25,000 with which to purchase and equip a radio station. In 1927, KGEF opened and Los Angeles was never the same again, a good portion of the town tuning in for Bob's nightly crusades.

Fighting Bob disdained most politicians, all lawyers but especially defense lawyers whom Bob called the real criminals, the YWCA for staging dances Saturday night that sometimes ran over into the Sabbath, and the Los Angeles Public Library which had, on its shelves, books not fit for "heathen China or anarchistic Russia."

Shuler didn't like Mayor Cryer and the mayor, usually unflappable, didn't like him. As Cryer's term ended, he sued Bob for libel. And, while the trial delighted the public, it failed to quell Fighting Bob. Similarly, the Knights of Columbus were outraged with Bob's rabid anti-Catholicism and they, too, sued, unfortunately to no successful result. In 1929, however, Bob tasted the lash.

In the summer of that year, both millionaire theater owner Alexander Pantages and his wife, Lois, had run afoul of the law. Lois had been charged with drunk driving. There had been an accident and a death. But, as she came to trial, Bob insisted loudly she'd never be given her just desserts since millionaires like Pantages bought the law. On the eve of the jury's verdict in the case, Bob told Los Angeles over the radio that he had evidence the jury had been fixed. When the jury came in with a guilty verdict, the Bar Association, another Shuler target of long standing, went after the preacher. He was charged with contempt of court and sentenced to thirty days in

The Honorable John R. Porter, mayor of the city of Los Angeles 1929–1933, teetotaler extraordinaire. In 1932, even his guests, Olympic big-wigs, had to be content to toast the opening of the Los Angeles Games with nonalcoholic beverages.

jail. He loudly protested he was being railroaded, though, in fact, he welcomed his martyrdom which he modestly compared to that suffered by the fathers of the church. Bob was one of the most pampered prisoners ever held in city jail. He got butter instead of margarine, tailored prison suits with tie, and reporters every day asking him how his ordeal was coming along. Even so, Bob elected to find a way to satisfy the court and get out early.

The peak of Bob's influence came in 1928 when he suggested that Los Angeles elect John R. Porter as its next mayor, and the city obliged. A former auto parts dealer — his foes dubbed him a junk man — Porter had served on the grand jury which indicted Marco and he thereby shared in the bounty from that kill. The highlights of Porter's regime included hosting the Olympics, the staging of which he had little to do with. The most memorable moment in his mayordom came

during a ceremonial visit to France. There his hosts insulted him by offering a toast in wine. Didn't France know Prohibition was on?

Porter granted Bob one of his wishes. Chief of Police Davis was demoted to the traffic detail and his subordinate, Strongarm Dick Steckel was elevated to the chief's chair.

But the quality of police work can't be said to have improved. The Walter Collins affair was a case in point. Mrs. Collins reported her son Walter missing. The police searched but were unable to find the boy. Months later, they summoned her and presented her with a lad they said was her son who had been located back East. She said he wasn't. The police insisted he was and that she take him home and try him out. She reluctantly did so but returned the boy saying he was definitely not her son. The police then charged she was guilty of "unnatural conduct" and imprisoned her in a psychiatric hospital. She

The murder of Charlie Crawford and Herb Spencer was the most sensational gangland shooting in Los Angeles' history, and the police did not have a clue.

was released when it turned out Walter had been murdered by a neighborhood boy.

Then there was the Jacobson case which had the pungency of Fish Harbor at San Pedro. One evening, reformer city councilman Carl Jacobson called on a constituent, Mrs. Callie Grimes, to talk about street lights. He wasn't inside long before a carload of police officers broke in. They were responding, they announced, to a report of a wild party in progress. They found, they said, the councilman with his pants down preparing to assault Mrs. Grimes. The councilman screamed frame.

Why had a captain and several lieutenants chosen to answer this call? Why had they made sure to take reporters with them? It appeared the cops had actually gotten to the Grimes' home before the councilman arrived. And the police swore that when Jacobson was arrested he was wearing only a red union suit and the councilman insisted his union suit was light gray. Then it turned out that Mrs. Grimes happened to be an in-law of one of the arresting officers.

Given the councilman's efforts to break the Crawford mob, it wasn't strange that someone was out to get him. Nor that they could use the LAPD as their vehicle of revenge. The Marco affair, the Jacobson case, Fighting Bob's forays, the crash of Julian Pete and the election of Mayor Porter convinced Charlie Crawford to take a vacation. Control of the organization passed to Stringbean McAfee or, more precisely, to his wife who was rumored to have the smarts in the family.

But Charlie, before long, missed his old gang. When he decided to return, he expected it would lead to trouble. Charlie announced he was back in an unorthodox manner. One Sunday in July, 1930, he attended services at St. Paul's Presbyterian Church and into the collection tray he dropped a diamond ring which he said was worth $3,500. It was his effort to get square with the Big Guy. However, the selection of St. Paul's for this act of charity was not fortuitous. The pastor at St. Paul's was the Reverend Gustave Briegleb who was Fighting Bob Shuler's right

Porter Defies Foes on Council

2¢ Daily Illustrated News 2¢

Volume 8, Number 297   Los Angeles, California, Friday, August 14, 1931   PHONE WH 1111   HOME DELIVERY 45¢ PER MONTH

FINAL EDITION

'I KILLED TO SAVE MY LIFE,' CLARK'S STORY

NEW PLANS ANNOUNCED BY MAYOR

Defying attempts of city council to get control of the commissioners which are placed under the mayor by the city charter, Mayor John C. Porter yesterday announced that in view of the council's decision to reject all appointments except those dictated by themselves, he would refuse to make any

Confident

CRAWFORD DREW GUN, SHOUTED TO SPENCER, 'GET HIM!' JURY TOLD

By E. F. P. COUGHLIN

David H. Clark, the only living witness to the crime, yesterday confessed that he killed Charles Crawford and Herbert Spencer last May 20. He shot both men in self-defense, Clark told a jury in Judge Stanley Murray's court, where he is on trial for Spencer's murder.

And the indirect reason for the dual slaying, declared the defendant, was his flat refusal to "frame" his "best friend," Chief of Police Roy E. Steckel."

Clark interrupted his long and moody monologue of events leading up to the shooting, when he stepped down from the witness stand, grasped the gun which despatched the fatal bullets, and gave his own version of the scene.

"I called Crawford a dirty skunk, and told him I would tell all the people what had occurred.

"He said, 'No ———— ever talked to me like that.'

"He pulled his gun out of his belt. I grabbed his right hand and held the gun parallel between us."

CAUGHT BY THROAT

"He caught me by the throat and called out, 'Get him, Herb!'"

Clark was speaking very slowly, spacing his words with dramatic effectiveness. Twenty feet away his wife sobbed convulsively.

Three hundred spectators, jammed into a space provided for 125, sat breathlessly on the edge of their seats.

Juror No. 4 fanned himself

Full Story of Shootings as Given on Stand

Following is the complete question and answer testimony of David H. Clark in direct examination yesterday:

Q—What is your name?
A—David Harris Clark.
Q—How old are you?
A—Thirty-three.
Q—How long have you lived here?
A—All my life.
Q—Were you born here?
A—Yes, I was born in Los Angeles.
Q—Does your family live here?
A—Yes, I have a father and mother and a wife here.
Q—When were you married?
A—Five years ago.
Q—What is your business occupation?
A—Attorney at law. I was admitted to practice in 1922.
Q—What school did you attend?
A—The University of Southern California.
Q—After you were admitted to practice, did you accept any official position?
A—Yes, I was appointed a deputy district attorney on July 1, 1922.
Q—And you remained as such until you resigned?
A—Yes.
Q—When did you resign?
A—I resigned March 1 of this year.
Q—Prior to March 1 of this year had you announced your candidacy for a municipal judgeship?
A—No, I resigned first and then announced my candidacy.

KNEW CRAWFORD CASUALLY

Admits Slayings

David H. Clark, on trial for his life, shown as he appeared on witness stand yesterday when he calmly told that he acted in self-defense when he shot Herbert Spencer and Charles Crawford.

—Daily News Photo

further appointments "for the present."

The mayor's action will extend the terms of all commissioners whose terms expired on July 1 indefinitely, and all will hold office until he decides to name their successors.

Unofficially, it was said that the action was taken in an effort to

Handsome Dave Clark walked into Charlie Crawford's Hollywood office armed and Charlie Crawford and newspaperman Herb Spencer ended up dead.

hand man.

Charlie got the publicity he expected and more since a public debate between Fighting Bob and his lieutenant followed. Bob insisted he'd as soon baptize a skunk as accept an offering from the likes of Charlie, while Briegleb argued for the charity of God while conceding the church's building fund had a deficit. Before long each minister, over the radio and in the newspapers, implored the Almighty to show his brother the errors of his ways.

In early 1931, a tribulation was visited on to Fighting Bob although the agency through which it was delivered was anything but supernatural. The Federal Radio Commission, precursor to the FCC, announced that it was going to take renewal of Bob's radio broadcasting license under consideration for what were alleged to be numerous abuses. Certainly Bob believed that the FRC's interest was spurred by the increasingly numerous and vitriolic attacks on him that appeared in Harry Chandler's *Times*.

The FRC hearings paraded Shuler's antagonists blasting away at their favorite target. The President of USC, Rufus von KleinSmid, insisted that the "monkey business" Bob charged was being taught on campus was only the theory of evolution. A beleaguered city health official denied he'd ordered medical inspections of women by men. One forum which had a heyday with this was the magazine *The Critic of Critics*.

The Critic of Critics featured articles lambasting Bob and his cronies and the best cheesecake photography in Los Angeles. It was founded, its editor, former newspaperman Herb Spencer, said, as a liberal voice in an ill-liberal city. In fact, the bankroll came from Charlie Crawford and one of *The Critic*'s favorite targets was Guy McAfee.

On the afternoon of May 20, 1931, *Critic* editor Spencer attended a meeting at the office of Charlie Crawford, on Sunset near Highland. There was a third party at that meeting who was not observed entering. But his departure was noted as he pulled out a gun and shot both Spencer and Crawford. The newspaperman got as far as the street, in pursuit of his assailant. Charlie

His honor da mayor of the city of Los Angeles, Frank Shaw, 1933–1938. Mayor Shaw was no fashion plate. He unfortunately adopted the trim little moustache he wore right at the moment they were being called Hitlerian.

Crawford died at the hospital. It was the most sensational gangland shooting in Los Angeles' history, and the police did not have a clue.

Los Angeles eagerly contemplated possible scenarios and elected favorite candidates for the murderer of the decade. The obvious candidate was McAfee but his alibi was airtight. At the time of the shootings, he'd been in the Hall of Justice.

The "who" who had done it topped the wildest speculation. Turning himself in was Handsome Dave Clark, a Deputy District Attorney and a candidate for a judgeship. Clark, the man who had prosecuted Marco, had, until now, a bright political future. His trial was impatiently awaited and the prosecutorial powers pushed it ahead. When Clark finally got a chance to tell Los Angeles his story, it was complete in all the details. Clark said he'd gone to see Crawford because of *The Critic*'s attacks. Crawford had changed the subject. He had asked Clark for help in luring Chief of Police Steckel to a dingy hotel in Santa Monica for the purposes of blackmail. Clark had righteously protested and that led to a war of words. Crawford threatened Clark so Clark drew a gun and shot both Crawford and Spencer.

Clark's story was maybe plausible. But probable or even likely? No, it was a bit too far-fetched. Little things were oddly wrong. Why had Crawford threatened Clark when he, Crawford, wasn't armed? Clark was the only one known to be carrying a rod that day. He insisted Crawford had had a gun but it had mysteriously disappeared.

There was another theory. Clark was no good guy. He had been, in fact, long associated with McAfee. If Clark had complained about attacks in *The Critic,* Crawford had probably just laughed and tried to persuade Clark to join him. When Clark refused, he did his talking with hot lead. How much the jury knew of this theory no one knows. They did know Clark was as good-looking as his nickname implied, that he made a good witness and that if he had killed L.A.'s number one hood so what? He'd done the town a favor. So the jury found Clark not guilty.

Later, in 1931, the FRC removed Fighting

Bob Shuler's broadcasting license and, after a tumultuous and unsuccessful campaign for U.S. Senator, Bob faded from the political scene. John Porter ran for re-election and was defeated by a county supervisor, Frank Shaw. And with Charlie Crawford dead, Guy McAfee happily pulled the strings operating Los Angeles vice. He found considerable cooperation downtown. The police department settled comfortably into its darkest hour, when appointments to the force and promotions within it were routinely bought and sold. The focus of civic power became a corner office at City Hall where Mayor Shaw had installed his brother Joe as major domo and chief fixer. To get anything done downtown, you had to speak "corner pocket language."

One of the few voices for reform was that of county supervisor John Anson Ford. Reacting to rumors of corruption at the county hospital, Ford asked a young restaurateur to undertake an investigation. Clifford Clinton was a fairly new arrival to Los Angeles where he'd opened his successful "cafeteria of the golden rule" — Clifton's.

Clinton investigated, showed the accuracy of the charges and, in the process, impressed Ford. Before long, Clinton, through Ford's good offices, found himself appointed to the county grand jury.

Clinton was not long in realizing that the grand jury could be an excellent pulpit, and he had a crusade in mind. He had heard charges that vice was protected in Los Angeles. So he walked through downtown to see if he could indeed place a bet or buy a woman. When it became obvious anyone could do both, and that such must be known to the police who chose to ignore it, he concluded vice was indeed protected. Clinton began a noisy campaign which thoroughly annoyed and irritated the Shaw administration.

The resources of an entrenched administration were considerable and, other than a great deal of public attention, Clinton was getting nowhere until January of 1938. On the morning of the 14th, a bomb blast shattered the automobile of private detective Harry Raymond. Unfortu-

Shows Motor Wrecked by Infernal Machine

DETECTIVE. LIEUT. LLOYD HURST points to the badly damaged motor in Harry J. Raymond's automobile. Raymond narrowly escaped death yesterday when a bomb exploded as he stepped on the starter in his garage, 955 Orme street. The force of the blast wrecked the automobile, shattered walls of the garage and sent Raymond to the hospital critically injured. Police believe Raymond was the target of an underworld plot.—Daily News Photo.

The bomb that tore apart Harry Raymond's car put over 150 pieces of shrapnel into his body, but he lived. An immigrant fruit vendor saw the bomb being planted and, despite a visit from the strongarm boys, insisted on telling his tale. It tore the cover off Angel Town, as the newspapers liked to say.

nately, Raymond was in the car at the time but, while he took over 150 pieces of shrapnel, he lived. The attempted assassination of Harry Raymond made big headlines, and the blast, as it was said, tore the lid off Los Angeles.

Raymond, an ex-cop who'd worked both sides of the street, had been investigating the Shaw administration for Ralph Grey, who was suing over an unpaid debt. Raymond was scheduled to testify when somebody tried to remind him his testimony wasn't wanted. Days later, that somebody was revealed and it created even more of a stir than the bomb itself. Raymond had been bombed by police lieutenant Earl Kynette who, with a secret police "spy squad," had had Raymond under surveillance for months.

The message to Raymond emanated from somewhere in City Hall. And it was all Clinton and his reformers needed to launch a recall against the Shaw administration. Through the summer of 1938, about all anyone in L.A. could hear about, read about, or talk about was the Shaw administration and the efforts to remove it from office. Hiz honor da mayor tried to remain aloof: "I am too busy with real work and real problems to give any thought to this curious combination of commercial advertising, poor sportsmanship, subversive activities and backfence gossip," he grandiloquently announced. This, while his minions beat up the opposition and churned out phony campaign literature in an attempt to discredit the reformers. "His Honor can wiggle his hips like a Notre Dame fullback," announced one reformer, "but he cannot untwist the incubus that is Kynette from his official neck."

On election day, Mayor Shaw was involuntarily retired, and the reform candidate, Judge Fletcher Bowron, elected. Earl Kynette went on trial, after having altered his appearance with a friendly moustache. He made sure he was never photographed without his wife and baby. Nevertheless, he was found guilty and sent to San Quentin. Police Chief Davis was involuntarily retired from office, not without having pled for help in retaining his job from a source as far away as J. Edgar Hoover.

The recall meant the end of Guy McAfee's L.A. career. He could read the handwriting on the wall and he looked around for some place where doing business was likely to be easier than Los Angeles. He found it in Las Vegas, and the remnants of the Crawford mob moved there.

As all this was happening, the big story came to be the threat of war and, if it came, what part Los Angeles would play. And, anyway, with the personalities who had heated up L.A. in the '20s and '30s gone, the civic sideshow just wasn't the spectacle it had once been.

Jack Doyle's Vernon bar was truly a
pleasure dome dedicated to strictly
male camaraderie and the appreciation
of good liquor. The only reminder
that there was a mundane world
outside was the sign Doyle had posted
(here visible at the center rear):
"Don't Buy Booze If The Baby Needs
Shoes."

5

PROHIBITION, OR, WHAT YOU MIGHT CALL THE SADDEST NIGHT OF ALL

To most people in Los Angeles, the night of June 30, 1919, didn't seem to be the saddest night in history. For a goodly number of Angelenos, it was just another midsummer evening and if anything about the date quickened the blood, it was anticipation of the coming July 4th holiday and a day off, a Red Car trip to the beach, perhaps. But for red-blooded Los Angeles, for two-fisted Los Angeles, there were no pleasing thoughts this evening. No, for virile Los Angeles, this night, Monday, June 30, 1919, was the night Prohibition finally came crashing down.

The events leading up to the sorry state of affairs began in 1913, when the Anti-Saloon League renewed its agitation against demon rum. There had always been an American prohibitionist movement of some kind or another but, fortunately, it had been ignored by the majority. But the chaos of the years immediately preceding the First World War had promoted many changes, and one was the idea that prohibition wasn't quite as irrational as it once had seemed. In turbulent 1917, a prohibitionist amendment to the Constitution finally passed Congress and, to the con-

sternation of the drinking public, the states signed on. Meanwhile, various forms of interim wartime prohibition were being proposed and one such measure finally passed. Ingloriously for Los Angeles, it was sponsored by local Prohibition Party Congressman Charles Randall. In November of 1918, President Wilson signed the bill into law. It was to take effect with the tolling of midnight, June 30, 1919.

Los Angeles had little to boast of in the struggle against intemperate temperance. Local red noses had long before lost the war to the blues. In 1917, by a majority of 20,000, the city had voluntarily placed upon itself the severest restrictions against alcohol of any major metropolitan center. Hard liquor sales were out, only beer and wine was allowed, provided they were of no greater than 14 percent alcoholic content. Even then, they could only be sold in public dining rooms which served "bonified" meals and only between the hours of 9:00 a.m. and 11:00 p.m. Booze was only to be had freely in the seamier districts, Chinatown or Little Italy, or across the city line in a small, independent municipality where liberality, and occasionally license, reigned, such as Venice or Vernon.

And very much so in Vernon. South and west of downtown Los Angeles, Vernon owed its existence to the foresight, perhaps cunning is a better word, of John Leonis. A Frenchman, Leonis arrived in the area in the 1880s, when there was nothing from the Los Angeles River to Alameda Street but vegetable farms. He opened a general store, worked hard and, like his adopted city, he prospered. One day, he was inspired to organize his neighbors in a move to withdraw from Los Angeles and incorporate as an independent city. The idea was to make the area attractive to manufacturing by manipulating land use through a locally elected city administration. Profits would accrue to those that owned the land. John Leonis and his friends, Vernon's first families, owned the land. In 1905, out of the beet fields arose, therefore, the city of Vernon. Its heart was very near the intersection of 38th Street and Santa Fe where John Leonis opened a bank. He was also voted onto the new city's council and he would remain there, without interruption, until he was carried out feet first some fifty years later.

Vernon's reputation as a drinking man's resort was the responsibility of John J. "Jack" Doyle. An ambitious Irishman, Doyle had worked on the Southern Pacific but had quit for the life of a sports promoter. He opened a small training camp for boxers in Arcadia, on the future site of Santa Anita Race Track. Before World War I, he had moved his operation to Vernon where, in addition to pugilism, he staged events like dog races. But it was the exhibitions of the sweet science that attracted an endless crowd of workingmen and, as the movies moved west, film celebrities, out to Vernon. Doyle's training camp was located at 38th and Santa Fe.

It was there that Doyle built a bar, a monumental edifice dedicated to inbibation. Inside were several bars, the greatest of which was advertised as the longest in the world. Thirty-seven bartenders poured on busy nights and the weekend take was never less than $20,000. This was not the sleazy alcoholic hell of anti-saloon agita-tion. Doyle had a reputation and he had sincerity, and over all his barroom was hung a sign which read: "DON'T BUY BOOZE IF THE BABY NEEDS SHOES." Now, on the night of June 30, 1919, all this was coming to an end.

It surprised no one that Vernon mourned the departure of King Brew in true bacchanalian fashion. Crowds estimated as high as 50,000 jammed 38th and Santa Fe. Drinking men were these, confronting the disturbing reality that, after midnight, they couldn't be sure where their next drink was coming from. The foot traffic spilled out into the streets and slowed the passage of the Yellow Cars of the Los Angeles Railway, arriving with thirsty reinforcements. Auto horns and an occasional saxophone filled the night. Bright lights illuminated the front of local liquor stores which were staying open until midnight and doing a brisk business. "THE UNITED STATES GOES DRY JULY 1," read the sign in one window, "BUY NOW TO LAST FOREVER."

In preparation for this night, Doyle had had the wall which separated his two largest bars knocked down and each bar was lengthened by fifteen feet. Still it wasn't enough as at least 1,000 men squeezed into the huge barroom, a crush described by one observer as "the completest and snuggest contacting of human beings one could imagine without consequences for the surgeon." Nobody was sure how many bartenders served this thirsty mass. Some said 60, others 200. What they couldn't drink they were taking home. Men left with their arms full, with suitcases roped shut, pushing wheelbarrows or struggling with an old sea chest packed to the gunnels.

Down the street from Doyle's, the last party was underway at the swank Vernon Country Club where the swells arrived in their Pierce-Arrows or Marmons. The club normally accommodated a few hundred. Tonight, cover was $2, tables were going for $50 each and, at the height of the festivities, 2,000 were packed in. The hottest jazz band in town was playing but who could hear or cared? Midnight was coming.

A long line of cars crowded the roads to Venice and special three-car trains of the Pacific Electric were in service to convey the estimated 100,000 drinking men and women who wanted to bid farewell to inebriation while at the sea. At the Ship Cafe alongside the Venice pier, tables were $300 each. Harlow's the Strand, the Ocean Inn and every other watering hole in Venice and neighboring Ocean Park locked their doors by 10:00 p.m. against the endless crush of revelers.

At midnight, there was "one grand crash of everything." Horns sounded, fireworks went off, lights swung crazily around in the sky: it was the 4th of July and New Year's Eve rolled together. Then, it was all over.

All over save for the hangovers which greeted many Angelenos upon arising on Day One of the Dry Era. If some were convinced that, judging from the way they felt, the world was coming to an end, they could draw some comfort in the second thought that they would be spared feeling as they did for a long time and perhaps forever. "You are lucky," wrote Dr. W. A. Evans gleefully and not without the smallest note of sarcasm. "Your troubles are over unless you are one of those rich men who have buried a few bones. Let us hope that you are blessed with poverty and that from now on you can get nothing stronger than buttermilk." For forcibly reformed alcoholics, the doctor suggested a diet of strained pears, strained farina, strained apple sauce, strained prunes and strained hominy grits, etc. and ad nauseam. Happy, happy, happy, the brave new world started with a strain.

A good deal was predicted by those who welcomed the change. Crime and domestic troubles, for example, were expected to decline. Consumption of candy and ice cream would rise dramatically, sweets filling the voids in stomachs around town. There would be increased spending on food and clothing because, after all, $20 million a year had been spent on alcohol and that money had to go somewhere. On the other hand, if you happened to be in the wine industry, you could expect to be out of a job. The great Californian wine fields, the *Times* reported, not unenthusiastically, would probably be ripped out.

One company, at Wineville, California, figured it would plant walnuts. And "Wineville," by the way, would be changed to Windsor. In Los Angeles, the Busch brewery would be converted to an ice house. Did L.A. really need that much ice?

And the people. The *Times* noted with fervor that "clergymen, educators and librarians predicted a higher standard of citizenship and intellectuality" generally among the masses. This turned out to be correct. A year after the onset of Prohibition, the *Times* reported that beer, whiskey, gin, brandies of every description, and even champagne, were being brewed in Los Angeles cellars and that all this activity represented dedication to and assiduous study of all available sources. "Every other man," the newspaper noted, "who was wont to use a brass rail as a footrest has a long list of recipes." The then current favorites were reported to involve sweet spirits of niter and an ice cream freezer. Another favored ingredient in home brews was "jake," Jamaican ginger. It had twice the proof of whiskey, tasted like carbolic acid, and was described by an admirer as "smell[ing] like somebody was shoeing horses." But a little jake could transform a glass of pallid cider into something with a real kick. A more professionally prepared product might include formaldehyde, wood alcohol and a dash of grape juice, just for color. Jake was sold at drug stores in two-ounce bottles. When the fact of its use became known, druggists informally rationed it, one bottle to a customer per night. Which meant that an evening's drinking involved constant interruptions while somebody ran out for a bottle purchased from a store located on an ever-widening circle of streets.

There were those, of course, who snorted in disgust at home brews, those whose material resources allowed them to lay in a private reserve. Uncle Tom McCarey was, like Jack Doyle, both a fixture in the local fight scene, and the owner of a liquor emporium, his on Washington Boulevard in Culver City. "Wine has always been the badge of aristocracy," Uncle Tom advertised. "In all ages the man of intellect and the connoisseur has used the products of the grape with a realization of their highly beneficial effects both physically and mentally." Before Prohibition, he prompted Angelenos to sit down and "list your requirements for future social affairs" and, amazingly enough, some did. One dedicated martini drinker was said to have calculated precisely the amount of his favorite liquor he liked to have each day, multiplied this by the number of days in a year and the years actuarially likely to be his, and made his purchase accordingly. Then again, there was the millionaire who purchased the complete stocks of two liquor stores, "including champagne which sells for $2 a bottle wholesale." No strained prunes required, nor wanted.

The day Prohibition broke out, Jack Doyle was asked if he thought the Great Experiment would work. "The idea is advanced that Los Angeles will settle down now and accept its condition of aridity with philosophy," he intoned. "Let no one imagine such a thing. People here . . . will continue to get what they have been used to from some source." Jack didn't worry one way or the other. He took his profits, invested them in oil strikes at Santa Fe Springs and became a rich man. His Vernon saloon never opened again.

As the dry decade wore on, it became obvious that it was anything but dry. Prohibition was something one read about in the *Times* or in the *Record* or the *Herald* or the *Examiner* when one or another newspaper was on the circulation warpath asking once again, Why Wasn't the Law Being Enforced? By the mid-1920s, according to the *Daily News*, the chain of illicit enterprises which combined to import liquor into Southern California was operating with "the minimum of interference" and little worry. Alcohol from around the world was being landed in Mexico and shipped up what was called the Bootleg Highway from Tecate to Tijuana to San Diego County. The road to Tecate was curiously well developed, curious when you consider that the surrounding countryside was pretty desolate and not farmed. Tecate itself hadn't been much to speak of, not before Prohibition hit the gringos

and a distillery was built in town. The stuff it turned out was 175 proof plus, intended as a base for bootleg gin, provided anyone could wait that long.

But the Bootleg Highway was the long way around. It was to sea that drinkers looked to slake their thirsts. The curvaceous, indented California coast was a smuggler's paradise. Smuggling had been big business since the days of the Spanish, and the American Coast Guard was just as hopelessly inefficient and outclassed as the Spanish authorities had been.

Who could take the enforcement fleet seriously when it consisted of vessels such as the sedentary *Vaughan*, a decrepit World War I subchaser, the last of its kind? Or how about the *Tamaroa*, a cutter, whose adroit performances at sea had earned her the nickname of "sea cow"? Or what about the *Bear*, a 52-year-old former Arctic ice breaker, the oldest vessel in American service? Eventually, eight smaller and faster patrol boats were added. Eight—to cover the entire coast from San Luis Obispo south to the Mexican border.

When one considers the geography of the California coast, it becomes apparent the gods seriously intended that Los Angeles drink. Islands, perfect shelters, are scattered about and, alongside the banks, excellent staging areas. From Cortes Bank off San Diego, Tanner Bank seaward from San Clemente Island, Osborne Bank in back of Santa Catalina, the enemy nightly gathered its forces. Larger vessels stood by and off-loaded their cargos onto a fleet of racy speedboats. Then began the dash to the coast, past an island like Catalina, where their high-powered engines were clearly audible. The Coast Guard was left behind. Los Angeles drank.

There were bootleggers in plenty and, where there were bootleggers, in the eyes of the newspapers, there had to be a king. There were numerous candidates: Tony or Frank Cornero, Ralph Shelton, Dominic Di Ciolla, Dick Scout, Walter South.

Let's take just one would-be king, Tony Cornero, who rose to even greater fame later as admiral of the rolling bones, captain of the gambling ship fleet which stood off the coastline after Repeal. Tony and his brothers bootlegged up and down the California coast, strict quality stuff from Canada, for the carriage trade. Why, Tony insisted later, one of his customers was none other than William Randolph Hearst who, while an absolute abstainer himself, nevertheless liked his guests at San Simeon to have the best of everything. Tony saw his career during Prohibition as one of public service, his only interest peddling the good stuff "to keep 120 million people from being poisoned to death."

Accounts of bootlegger wars were good circulation builders for the newspapers. Hijackings were common occurrences and were often accompanied by an exchange of hot lead. Bootleggers ran considerable risks and some of that risk even came from the forces of law and order.

On the evening of May 30, 1924, Tony, alias Earl Moore, alias Tony Michaels, was out on a delivery. He drove his late-model Lincoln touring car down Hobart Avenue and stopped in front of number 150. He was accompanied by Ben Oaken, who had as many aliases as Tony, and twenty cases of Scotch whiskey, to be delivered at $57.20 a case.

What Tony did not know was that the man who lived at 150 and who'd placed the order, had, for whatever reasons, passed the information along to the police. At the moment Tony rang the doorbell, two of the boys in blue were waiting inside. Tony's client opened the door and led him toward the back. Outside the closed door to the breakfast room, he stopped and pointed. "Go in there and collect your money," he said. Tony knew instantly something was up. He pulled out two gats and yelled "To hell with you!" and the shooting started. After the smoke had cleared, Tony had taken two slugs and one of the coppers had a bullet in the thigh. For all this, Tony got a fine of $300. Neither lead nor the law slowed Tony's style.

A more serious contretemps occurred two years later when Tony was busted on his yacht the *Donnarsari* with 1,000 cases of good whis-

Above right. Where liquor violations got you in the bad old days, ca 1925 — the interior of the Lincoln Heights jail.

key. This was an affront the law could not suffer lightly. For this infraction, Tony was dished two years in the Federal hostelry at McNeil Island, Washington.

Tony did not, however, begin serving his time right away. What happened isn't clear. The story Tony liked to tell in later years was that, while being transported aboard a train to Washington state, he excused himself to go to the bathroom and kept on excusing himself out the window. Whatever the method used, Tony spent the next few years a fugitive from justice.

At one point, Internal Revenue Service agents were sure Tony was in hiding just across the Mexican border. Knowing the close relationship that existed between the FBI and the Mexican authorities, the IRS agent in Los Angeles approached his opposite at the Bureau with a plan. Couldn't it be suggested to the Mexicans that they quietly apprehend Tony, escort him to the border and there give him a swift kick in his rights? The FBI agent enthusiastically passed the plan along to J. Edgar Hoover, who politely and officially declined to take part.

The next matter which came to Federal attention and which involved Tony concerned the ship *Premzyl*. She was ostensibly operated by a German syndicate and had been loaded in Holland with half a million dollars in first-class liquors. Her destination was the Ventura coast where she was to arrive in the dead of night.

The Feds knew all this because the captain

of the *Premzyl* sailed her instead into New Orleans harbor and surrendered his ship. He had no intention of being a party to a violation of American law and, in any case, a generous reward was being offered by the government for the surrender of contraband cargos. But before he could collect, lawyers for the owners surfaced demanding the captain's arrest. He was, they insisted, guilty of barratry, the willful redirection of a ship at sea by her master in violation of his orders. Federal officials were forced to hand the captain over to German authorities and the ship was set free, cargo intact.

The *Premzyl* was trailed by the Coast Guard as she left port headed toward the West Coast. She shook her tail somewhere off California. The next that was seen of the *Premzyl*, she was steaming into Los Angeles harbor minus her cargo. The government, suspecting that the cargo was, at that moment, being imbibed by local residents, seized the ship for nonpayment of import taxes. It was not long before the government was convinced that the man behind the *Premzyl* was Tony Cornero.

In late 1929, Cornero strolled casually into the downtown Los Angeles offices of Internal Revenue Service agent S. H. Hamer and announced his desire to get square with the law. He professed ignorance of the government's efforts to find and talk with him. He insisted he was "out of the rackets" and wanted to make good: "My family's here and I want to do some-

thing worthwhile." That, as far as the government was concerned, was to serve the balance of his prison term. Next, Tony could pony over $307,227.41, which the government figured it was owed on the *Premzyl*'s cargo.

Prohibition drove the price of alcohol up, at first. Real beer went up to 75¢ a quart, whiskey to 25¢ a shot, and wine was $3–$5 a quart, f.o.b. in Little Italy. Prices rose steadily until a sub rosa brewing and importing empire was in place, then prices began to fall. By 1930, prices were downright depressed. A gallon of raw alcohol was going for $4, $20 for the economy-size, five-gallon tin whereas it had been anywhere between $45 and $75 for five gallons. Bourbon was now $19–$26 a case at the wholesale level, that is at the rail off Catalina, and $35–$45 on shore. Scotch, which had never known Scotland, was $22 a case; there was no charge for the authentic-looking labels or bottles in which it was packed.

Times were tough. While Tony was vacationing behind bars, his brother Frank had to increase the business to 500 cases a week, with a commensurate increase in risk, just to make a profit. Pity poor Thum Mankin, who set out from San Francisco to Los Angeles with a ship loaded with 80,000 cases of whiskey, only to collide in a fog with another southern-bound rumrunner. The coastal crush for what business there was was appalling.

So, one way or another the booze was getting through. It was even available at restaurants where, if the waiter knew you, you could get two fingers worth, at ice cream parlors where the sundaes were loaded, and at drug stores where medicinal bitters were sold by the shot, at 75¢ per. Blind pigs and speakeasies abounded.

There was no mistaking the Pink Rat on Alvarado. Those in the know realized it was named after the infamous Rat Mort of Paris, "a notorious vice den." And if one wasn't in the know, wasn't wise to the ways of the world, it was possible to learn of such places courtesy of the Rev. Gustave Briegleb of nearby Westlake Presbyterian Church, a well-known sermonizer on matters relating to the body politic. When Dr.

If you remember Bernie's, it probably wasn't because of his corned beef, but because the deli served as a "speak." A newspaper reporter bought the stuff and then ungraciously sent a photographer to grab a picture. The next day everybody in Los Angeles knew what they already knew: that the liquor laws were being broken.

FLOTSAM —By Dorman Smith

The editorial viewpoint of the *Daily News* on the illegal, nightly importation of alcohol into Los Angeles. What is the meaning of the skulls? Certainly not booze brigadiers crushed in the surf. Then, imbibers? Perish the thought!

Briegleb informed his congregation that, in gazing upon the Pink Rat, one "would immediately know that its very appearance indicated a place which has to be given over to the world, the flesh and the devil," all matters fortunately covered by the eighteenth amendment, Police Chief Lyle Pendergast obligingly raided and closed the place. The Pink Rat, the newspapers reported, had been "bleached white by the processes of the law."

There's no record of anything more athletic than elbow-bending ever having transpired at the Vernon Country Club. The Club enjoyed a quiet reputation until the morning it was catapulted into general notoriety when an account of what went on there was splashed across the front page of the *Times*, in space customarily reserved for international malfeasance and the grisliest of murders.

"Whiskey, Women, make Jazzy Night at Club," read the headline. By jazz the "muscle-tickling kind" was meant. The denizens of this muscle-tickled inferno were scantily dressed young women who smoked cigarettes with absurdly long holders and stared out at their beaus through thick makeup. The men's coats were smudged with powder from "encircling the creamy bared shoulders of fairies in evening gowns."

Everywhere was alcohol. Pints were $16 each. The floor was covered with empty bottles, the management presenting no objection to patrons packing their own. Liberality bred license. Dark-eyed women openly encouraged panting youths. One blonde was showing off her frontal exposure when a male companion decided to add to the demonstration by seizing her spaghetti straps and forcibly lowering her gown a few extra inches.

Those Angelenos who missed reading of these licentious goings-on heard about it the following Sunday from the town's master dispenser of hellfire and brimstone, the Reverend Bob Shuler, fortuitously newly arrived in town. The sermon which introduced him to his new city-wide congregation was entitled "The Vernon Country Club vs. Decency: Will Los Angeles Stand for It?"

The way Shuler saw it, the *Times* had been entirely too polite in its account. The women at the V.C.C. were: "cigaret-smoking, wine-drinking, semi-nude slobbering women of the underworld." Back where he came from (the Cumberland Gap by way of Texas), a real lady would no more be found in such a place than she would have "voluntarily hugged to her bosom a mountain rattler." And, if Bob was not making his views clear, he assured his audience that "the sooner modern society leaves off the paint and dance and cigaret and booze of the brothel, the surer American civilization will be saved from the pit of the damned."

Everyone but the unreconstituted led by Fighting Bob Shuler had long realized Prohibition was a flop. The unreconstituted insisted only diligent enforcement was needed. Wiser heads realized that violation of the liquor laws was as unchecked among the police as it was among the population at large. One police chief, Louis D. Oakes, hero of the Witherell kidnapping, was arrested in delecto flagrante in San Bernardino, and with an open bottle of hootch. The *Times* adopted the logic that, as much as one might disagree with the law, it was, after all, part of the Constitution and no right-minded citizen dared disobey the Constitution. Implicit in the *Times'* stance was the realization that the very best classes in society were as unresponsive to the law as those more familiar with illegal behavior. And this being the case the law was doomed.

And eventually, not with a bang but with a whimper, Gandier, Wright, Volstad, the local, state and national ordinances respectively, disappeared from the statute books. Goodbye and good riddance. But consider the plight of poor Everett Mack. He was arrested after the statewide Wright Act had been repealed by the voters, but before the formalities had been complied with and the law stricken from the books. The courts ruled the bust was good. He was fined $200. There was some solace in that, by the time he had paid his fine, he could forget all about it over a few drinks at his newly reopened neighborhood bar.

Tony Cornero's pride, the flagship of
the gambling fleet, the *Rex* under
siege by the forces of law and order,
in Santa Monica bay, August, 1939.

6

SPORTIVE GAMES AND OTHER AMUSEMENTS AFLOAT: THE GAMBLING SHIPS

In 1928, the outfitting of the ship *Johanna Smith* was announced at Long Beach. She had been a carrier in the lumber trade and now she was to be a "floating dance pavilion and cafe," to be anchored off Long Beach.

The *Johanna Smith* that was finally launched turned out to be something else again. With one roulette wheel, three crap tables, three blackjack tables, two chuck-a-luck cages, twenty-three slot machines which took from 5¢ to $1, but sans a dance floor, the *Johanna Smith* was no pavilion, she was a floating casino. She was the ship that launched the era of the gambling ships and she was one thing more: a constant source of annoyance and embarrassment to impotent law-enforcement agents.

The name of the genius who dreamed up the idea behind the *Johanna Smith* is lost. What he had done, however, was to discover how to float a bulky ship in a strange chink in the law. Gambling was very illegal in the state of California. The jurisdiction of the state extended, however, only three miles out to sea. After that, the *Johanna Smith* was required to obey Federal law. And, there was no Federal statute against gambling on the high seas. There was a law against crooked gambling, an outgrowth of the luxury trans-Atlantic liners and their well-heeled passengers who disliked being fleeced by aquatic card sharks.

When the occupation of the *Johanna Smith* became known, the law did what it could. The ship was seized, towed to port and her gambling paraphernalia inspected. It was found to be operating honestly. There being nothing further the law could do, the ship was turned loose and returned to her haven at sea. From there, her lights beckoned, an open invitation to red-blooded Angelenos to journey out the few short miles and try their luck.

The *Times* was infuriated at the appearance of the *Johanna Smith*: "If the gamblers were to work as hard at something constructive as they do at schemes to reduce the public purse, they might qualify as our most eminent and wealthy citizens." The newspaper was sure: "The masterminds chose the wrong coast. Long Beach has always been noted for its morality and sobriety.

The dictionary defines "sportive" as gay, frolicsome and not serious. But Los Angeles knew that the sportive games in this 1932 ad meant the very serious kind which involved a pair of dice or revolved around a roulette wheel.

The criminal class has never felt at home there. . . . The law will always get them in the end."

Long Beach city fathers leveled what they were sure would be a fatal blow to the ship. Water taxis were necessary to convey the sporting-minded to the ship. The city council passed an ordinance making it illegal for a taxi to convey anyone to anyplace where "immoral acts" were taking place. The owners of the *Johanna Smith* successfully argued in court that it was no more illegal for a water taxi to go to the ship than for a land-based taxi to go to Las Vegas or Tijuana. The courts agreed. Obviously, the end was not yet.

The success of the *Johanna Smith* bred competition. The *Monfalcone* had been built in Texas and had, in 1923, broken up in a storm, giving her the reputation of being a "hoodoo," a jinx ship. When she opened as a gambling barge in 1928, the hex was on the bettors. In 1930, a mysterious fire burned the ship to the water line. Three hundred and fifty patrons had to be rescued. While being towed to port, the hull of the ship sank. Days later, divers went after the ship's safe. They found it, the door wide open and the contents, $50,000, missing.

The *Johanna Smith* suffered a similar fire in 1932. It's not impossible that it was set by underworld antagonists. In July of 1935, six men armed with automatic weapons seized the *Monte Carlo,* yet another gambling ship, chained up the crew and robbed the passengers of $35,000 in cash and jewels. Months later, the case was cracked, the cash recovered and some of the jewels as well. They had been hidden in a hollowed-out bedpost. The life of the gambling ships was not all smooth sailing.

Passengers definitely boarded the ships at their own risk. Aboard the *City of Panama* one night, a frisky patron staged an impromptu show which, while amusing, drew customers from the tables. When he persisted despite the suggestions of the management, bouncers worked him over. He died. "Evidently the truculence that comes from repeated lawbreaking and getting away with it," editorialized the *Daily News,* "car-

ried the gambling ship bouncers too far. If the passenger gets too frisky, knock him on the head and throw him overboard is the code of the modern pirate." The bouncers were arrested but eventually found not guilty.

The ships drew well-heeled slummers and the underclasses, and the mix of the two created a charged atmosphere aboard the dank ships. Raymond Chandler caught it when his character Philip Marlowe visits a ship in *Farewell, My Lovely.* Paul Cain's *Fast One* is equally compelling. The *Johanna Smith,* the *Monfalcone,* the *City of Panama* (later the *City of Hollywood*), the *Monte Carlo,* the *Texas,* the *Showboat,* and S.S. *La Playa*: the ships were popular, and they operated from Long Beach north to Santa Monica, year after year.

They were certainly unforgettable to John Law who never tired in his efforts to shut them down. Use of the Federal anti-smuggling laws was heatedly suggested by a newspaper. A Federal official was forced to point out that anti-smuggling laws could only be invoked where smuggling was going on. The "Al Capone treatment" was proposed: get 'em on tax violations. Except the owners of the ships paid their taxes scrupulously. After all, they contended they were in a perfectly legal business so why shouldn't they? Another inspired attack involved invoking the quarantine laws and segregating returning passengers until they showed they were free of plague. Somebody somewhere doubted that one was Constitutional.

The simplest way of shutting down the ships would have been for Congress to outlaw gambling in Federal jurisdiction. That was strongly fought by the fishing industry. Not that they had any sympathy for the ships, they just felt that, if the government got involved in this, it would be used as a precedent for future Federal intervention in their industry.

In 1930, having served time for violating the Prohibition laws, Tony Cornero Stralla emerged from prison. With Prohibition on the verge of repeal, Tony had to find another and hopefully as profitable line of work. He became partnered in the gambling ship *Tango,* then floating off Long Beach. As Tony liked to tell the story, doubtlessly considerably embellished, he didn't see eye to eye with his partner. Tony suggested one throw of the dice, winner take all. Tony lost.

It was only a temporary setback. Tony had in mind opening his own ship, something much grander than any to date. He paid $150,000 for an old British collier built in 1887, the *Kenilworth.* Under that name, she'd proudly worked the trade routes between the United States and England and had once held a speed record. As *The Star of Scotland* she'd been part of the Alaskan salmon fleet. But when Tony found her, she'd been reduced to duty as a fishing barge off Santa Monica.

He put $250,000 into her, removing her engines and installing electrical generators. Lifeboats for 1,600 were placed aboard. Her superstructure was sheared away and a wooden shed erected along the deck giving her an ark-like appearance.

There were two decks on the refurbished *Rex,* as Tony decided to call his ship. The lower featured a dining room presided over by a notable chef and a bingo parlor which seated 500. There were two games every hour for a jackpot of $50 and one each night for $500. During the day, the bingo room served for pool and off-track betting where Racing Forms and scratch sheets were distributed free of charge. Racing information was secretly beamed aboard via a converted dentist's diathermy machine.

The main action took place on top. The main deck was richly paneled in wood and contained a saloon 250 feet long by 40 feet wide. On one side was a bar and facing it were the slots, 300 of them. Between the two were six roulette wheels, six chuck-a-luck cages, eight dice tables, a Chinese lottery (keno) with a $4,000 payoff, and a faro bank which Tony sometimes dealt personally.

In early May, 1938, the impending opening of the *Rex* was announced. Tony wasn't going to launch any ship of his in the middle of the night. Airplanes inserted the ship's name into the skies above Los Angeles and big ads were inserted into

Tony Cornero in his prime, a good man with the law books.

the papers. "OPEN MAY 5th, and every afternoon and evening thereafter. Cocktail bar. No cover. Popular priced meals at all hours. Cuisine by Battista, formerly of Trocadero and Victor Hugo's — ALL THE THRILLS OF BIARRITZ, RIVIERA, MONTE CARLO, CANNES — SURPASSED." And the beauty of it was it was only minutes from Hollywood.

Tony Cornero now demonstrated he was an inspired manager of gambling. He realized the big profits weren't to be made from either the well-to-do or the big gamblers, but from the masses of middle-class folks who could be coaxed aboard to play the slots or roulette. They demanded clean, attractive, well-run premises, and this Tony provided. It was a lesson Las Vegas learned from Tony Cornero.

"We don't want it!" thundered the *Santa Monica Evening Outlook,* shaking its editorial fist against the interloper. "The gambling barge *Rex*

The gambling ship S.S. *Monte Carlo,* a floating mint, at sea in the early 1930s.

will be no asset to Santa Monica," the newspaper asserted. Mayor E. S. Gillette was under considerable pressure to do something. Finally, he settled on forbidding Tony to have a brass band on the Santa Monica Pier the day the ship opened.

Needless to say that darkened the day not at all. The *Rex* opened to appreciative crowds. A fleet of thirteen water taxis was kept busy ferrying people back and forth. The *Rex* was open twenty-four hours a day, and there were seldom less than a 1,000 people aboard, and 2–3,000 during the peak hours.

"There will always be a full crop of squirrels in the world," declared Tony, squirrels being his not unaffectionate name for his customers. Squirrels weren't suckers as far as Tony was concerned. A squirrel was "looking only for fun, entertainment. And that's what I give him."

Tony was a master at public relations. When a local minister started stirring up anti-*Rex* feelings, Tony invited him aboard for a chat. He fed the minister a meal, showed him around, and suggested installing an almsbox immediately next to the slots, the contributions to benefit the man's church. "Help us that we may help," read the sign over the box. "Charity bringeth its own reward."

From time to time, the rumor spread that the games aboard the ships were rigged. Tony would have none of that. He entered the following in local newspapers:

NOTICE! TO WHOM IT MAY CONCERN:

I, TONY CORNERO STRALLA, agent for the S.S. *Rex,* anchored three miles off Santa Monica Pier, do hereby challenge any movie or radio star, sponsor or broadcasting station, newspaper or any other person or persons to find on board the *Rex* any illegally or crookedly operated games.

If anyone, and I mean ANYONE, can find aboard the S.S. *Rex* a falsely run game, then I will pay to that person or persons the sum of ONE HUNDRED THOUSAND DOLLARS ($100,000) cash on demand.

The S.S. *Rex* is run honestly and aboveboard and is operated by courageous, openminded, fearless American citizens.

— TONY CORNERO STRALLA
Agent S.S. *Rex*

Tony restricted the house take, the portion of each dollar wagered the house kept, to 1.4 percent. Of every dollar bet, 98.6 cents was returned in winnings. Tony said this was lower than the take in Vegas. "We are an asset to the merchants who are doing all the kicking," Tony said, "we make money circulate."

As low as the take was, owning the *Rex* was the next best thing to owning a mint. It was estimated as much as $400,000 was wagered on a busy night of which the house would keep about $6,000. Of that $4,500 would go to overhead. Another estimate put Tony's daily profit closer to $10,000 a day. He was making somewhere between a half million and a million dollars a year.

Cornero was a master of casino operation. He used shills, but subtly. Attractive young women were hired to circulate through the casino. When they spotted an empty table, they were instructed to go there and play. For this the ladies received $5 a shift.

The ship's bouncers weren't the goons other ships employed. They were mess-jacketed and polite. Their chief, a hulk of a man they called The Deacon, was the master of the discreet bump when it looked like a customer might be carrying a gun. Guns were forbidden aboard the *Rex*.

The customer was catered to in every way. The *Rex* even took checks, and a former official of the American Bankers Association was employed to approve them. Meals were reasonable. The water taxi service practically free.

The law never ceased gnashing its teeth over the continuing, uninhibited play aboard the gambling ships. In the summer of 1938, District Attorney Buron Fitts once again decided to try and shutter the fleet. It might have been that his moral sense was rubbed raw. On the other hand, in the political tumultuous days of that summer leading up to the city's recall of Mayor Frank Shaw, Fitts may have sensed hay was to be made attacking the ships. With Fitts, it was not always easy to establish his motivation although self-interest was never to be excluded.

So it was that Fitts, accompanied by Sheriff Eugene Biscailuz and a Santa Monica police chief with the unfortunate name of Dice, crept down to the Santa Monica Pier, seized the water taxi fleet, and ordered a course for the *Rex*. The law did not appreciate the close relationship between the taxi captains and Tony. So when one taxi sounded its horn, Tony was tipped off as to what was up. Guards aboard the *Rex* slammed an iron gate down over the ship's landing platform, denying access to the ship, keeping the law at bay in the bay.

Protracted negotiations followed during which the water taxi captains kept their boats sideways to the surf, calculated to cause the landlubbers the maximum amount of discomfort. Finally, a deal was cut whereby Tony allowed Fitts aboard and submitted to arrest in order to test the *Rex*'s legality.

That the raid was a comic opera affair did not escape note in the press. "So smooth was the raid accomplished," a newspaper commented, "that none of the gambling was interrupted." Fitts insisted he'd win in the courts, but if he didn't he righteously declared, he'd "blow up the tub myself."

The issue to be decided by the courts revolved around whether the *Rex* was in fact within the jurisdiction of the state of California. To be outside the state, the ship had to be more than three miles from shore. The shore is not, of course, a straight line. And where the coast formed a bay, to be outside that bay, a ship, under the law, had to be anchored three miles beyond an imaginary line drawn between the headlands of the bay, in this case Point Vicente and Point Dume.

The argument was no quaint point of law to Tony. If the *Rex* was required to be outside Santa Monica bay, it would have to move to a position miles out to sea, far beyond the convenient three miles from the pier the ship was enjoying. Neither the *Rex* nor its customers were seaworthy enough for so remote a station.

Tony argued, brilliantly, that the *Rex* didn't have to move since Santa Monica bay was no bay at all and never had been. It was, simply, a bight, a big identation in the coastline. To support his money. Then, in the summer of 1939, storm clouds appeared.

Or a storm cloud, in the person of State Attorney General Earl Warren. In July, Warren called the gambling ships "a great nuisance . . . drawing millions of dollars annually from legitimate channels. If we can have gambling ships anchored off our coast, we can have houses of prostitution and narcotics dives anchored off our coast." Warren told the press his visit was occasioned by a desire to see the ships out of operation.

Things were different politically in 1939 than they'd been a year earlier. There was a new reform-minded mayor in office and a new police chief. And Warren had a new tactic in mind.

On Friday, July 28th, Warren served the four gambling ships then operating, the *Tango,* the *Showboat,* the *Texas* and the *Rex,* with nuisance abatement orders. The order charged that the ships were a nuisance for a long list of reasons. First was that they "induce people to lead idle and dissolute lives." Warren was basing his action on a little-tested argument in law that a state had the power to abate a nuisance, even though the source of that nuisance was outside its immediate jurisdiction.

On August 2, the ships having refused to shut down, Warren commandeered the ships of the state's Fish and Game Department and staged a series of lightning raids. The *Texas,* the *Showboat* and the *Tango* were captured immediately. The *Rex* once again sensed the impending action, slammed down its portals and, training a fire hose on the besiegers, barred their access. A stand-off followed.

Warren was jubilant. The score as far as he was concerned was 4-0. "We've made good our promise to close the gambling ships," stated the Attorney General, "If we don't arrest all the operators and the dealers and all the others responsible for this appalling situation tonight, we'll get 'em tomorrow. Or we'll starve them out." Tony shouted back his defiance from the deck of his beleaguered ship: "If I go off it'll be in a box," he said.

Tony Cornero (right) proving his case that Santa Monica bay was no bay, but merely a bight, 1938.

contention, Tony introduced into court maps going back fifty years none of which called the bay a bay. A marine insurance agent, a Naval officer, the captain of the Port of Santa Monica, and two master mariners all obligingly offered their confirmation that the bay was no bay at all. The lower court ruled against Tony. But the Appeals Court reversed that decision and handed down the startling judgement, startling certainly to residents of the Santa Monica bight cities, that the bay was no bay.

For the next year, the *Rex* was open and jumping, and operating conveniently close to shore, going nowhere and making a great deal of

When law and order finally took over the *Rex*, their victory was celebrated by the hasty disposal of the ship's gambling machinery. Gambling ship owners charged they had been attacked by pirates, but the courts didn't agree.

Now began the epic Battle of Santa Monica Bay as it was dubbed by the wags in the press. For the next week, the stalemate in Santa Monica bay drove the international news off the front page, as Los Angeles rolled in mirth at the mock-heroic antics. Cornero was only too delighted to engage in verbal fencing with the law as it bobbed around the *Rex* or shoot out a quip or two to a floating reporter. The law, stymied, held out. After all, the *Rex* has no engines and so an offer could be made that the ship was free to sail away.

Suddenly, on the eighth day, it was over. Cornero came ashore and surrendered. He had plenty of provisions he told reporters, he had everything he needed for an extended stay. Except a barber, and now he needed a haircut.

The law's revenge was swift and Los Angeles was treated to endless photographs of the seized ships being ransacked, their gambling paraphernalia being tossed into the sea. Piracy the ship owners called it, especially since as far as the law went, the ruling still stood that Santa Monica was a bight and not a bay.

Charges were never pressed against Tony. The courts upheld Earl Warren's right to act as he had and the State Supreme Court eventually recalled Santa Monica from the ranks of the bights and reinstated it as a bay. The approach of war drove the final spike in the coffin of the *Rex*. Tony Cornero would be heard from again, after the war, when he returned with yet another scheme for ocean-going gambling. But it didn't include the poor *Rex*. She went to war and was eventually captured by a German submarine and sunk off the coast of Africa.

The Town of Make-believe

There is a town of make-believe
Where Hollywoodians live.
In seeming something they are not
Their precious time they give.

Their faces look like other folk
With paint and powder changed,
To seem like pictures in a book
Their costumes are arranged.

A caveman or a bathing maid
May meet you in the street,
Or Roman soldier all aglare
With armor quite complete.

A stranger in this funny town
Will think he's had a dream.
Until he looks around to find
Things are not what they seem.

—Anonymous Pro-Hollywood Poet

7

GLAMOROUS HOLLYWOOD: THE HOME OF THE STARS AND EVERYONE ELSE

Touring Los Angeles in the '20s, there was plenty to remind you you were in Hollywood. Looming above the Echo Park area were the shattered remains of an English three-masted sailing ship, abandoned there when the film in which it had sailed weighed anchor and sank. The towers Doug Fairbanks swung from in *The Thief of Bagdad* mournfully guarded Santa Monica Boulevard. Even D. W. Griffith's fanciful Babylon, constructed for *Intolerance* complete with hanging gardens, remained, crumbling, near Sunset and Western, a generation after the film had been forgotten.

Los Angeles was always in two minds about Hollywood. The city gleefully accepted the stack of dollars film production added to the local economy, but no one was wild about film people, whose hair-brained antics and slippery morality cast aspersions on Los Angeles' good name. Similarly, Los Angeles was delighted with the profits Hollywood tourism brought in, but was lukewarm about the tourists themselves, especially those who came intent on breaking into film biz. But the suburb's biggest sin was that, in time, it

was almost as well known as Los Angeles itself which meant the tail was wagging the dog.

A small irony was that the first movies made here were shot in downtown Los Angeles, the first set having been constructed on top of a Chinese laundry on Olive Street. L.A. officially never took notice, whereas Hollywood later erected not one, but two plaques within its purlieu. In Hollywood, they would never send anyone away disappointed.

The first full-scale production facilities were east and north of downtown L.A. in the Edendale district, off Glendale Boulevard, where Mack Sennett created a funny farm which housed the Keystone Kops. On the east side, Louis B. Mayer founded his Metropolitan Pictures, just down the street from the most famous early movie landmark of them all, Colonel William Selig's zoo. Tourists thought the Selig zoo was the city zoo but it was simply a home for animal extras. The first Tarzan found his first mate here, this in a day when the luxuriant hillsides could pass, with a minimum of dressing, for far-off Africa.

Claudette Colbert checks out her portrait along Santa Claus Lane, as Hollywood Boulevard temporarily became each Christmas. The decorations are courtesy of Otto K. Oleson.

While this was going on downtown, a world away there was Hollywood, which, as far as the Hollywoodians of that day were concerned, was a center of culture and civility and calm, mostly calm. It was set well apart from the hurly-burly of downtown. After Tunnel Day, 1909, the community was linked by Pacific Electric Red Car to the hub of business. In the popular Hollywood Line's heyday, cars left the Hill Street station every ten minutes, and, in the mid-1920s, close to 17 million passengers were being accommodated each year. It was one of the system's few profitable lines.

There was one vital thing Hollywood lacked: water. When Los Angeles developed its famous aqueduct, it made the city an offer it could not afford to refuse. Take the water practically free. Only disincorporate as an independent municipality and merge into Los Angeles. This Hollywood did with nary a whimper. In 1910, Hollywood formally ceased to exist and, in its place, was substituted just another Los Angeles neighborhood.

A year later, David Horsley of the Nestor Film Company arrived from the East Coast. An acquaintance who lived in Hollywood introduced him to Mrs. Blondeau, who had owned a tavern at the corner of Sunset and Gower. It had been put out of business when the upright citizens of Hollywood had voted in Prohibition. In an excess of moral zeal, they'd also refused to allow the keeping of hotels or restaurants in their community since both, along with bars, especially bars, attracted the wrong kind of people. Mrs. Blondeau's revenge upon a staid citizenry was to rent the shell of her tavern to Horsley for a studio for his film company, thereby launching the winning combination which was Hollywood and the movies.

Hollywood was quickly aware of what had come to pass. Keystone Kops and their hundred imitators were soon chasing one another over back fences, through carefully laid-out gardens, over well-tended lawns, all for the camera. Any intersection was fit for an impromptu car stunt or two. If a crowd was needed for a shot, the sidewalk was cordoned off and bystanders press-ganged into a movie debut. Nobody cared much. This was a day when no official permission was required for such mayhem.

Robin Hood swung through the trees just north of Hollywood, and Custer's Last Stand was repeated in a hollow that later became Silver Lake Reservoir. D. W. Griffith staged the Civil War in North Hollywood. The Valley, over the hills from Hollywood, was good for practically anything, including Pontus, the legendary land of the Amazons. When a massive battle of the sexes was staged there, 160 were injured, mostly women. "A tree is a tree," the saying went, "shoot it in Griffith Park" which film-makers were sure was named after D.W. himself.

In 1915, "Uncle" Carl Laemmle opened his massive Universal City. The facility was the inspiration for many stories. Laemmle had, it was said, convinced the Secretary of the Navy into allowing the Navy to sail up the Los Angeles River to fire a salvo in salute. That the Los Angeles River was a dry bed crimped the story not at all.

The Warner Brothers opened their studio at the eastern end of Hollywood, in the middle of a field on Sunset. It was there a good part of *The Jazz Singer* was later made. Vitagraph had facilities on Prospect near Sunset, the lot later passing over to Warner Brothers and then to the American Broadcasting Corporation. Jesse Lasky created a large lot around a barn near the corner of Sunset and Vine and, slightly north of there, Cecil B. De Mille shot *The Squaw Man.*

What happened was that Hollywood's fame grew and grew and, as a result, the map of Los Angeles literally was reworked. Remember Lankershim and Toluca? They disappeared off the map and together became North Hollywood, although Toluca was revived years later for Bob Hope's development of Toluca Lake. What became of Ivanhoe and Prospect Park? No romance there and they were transformed into plain East Hollywood. Colegrove had been named by the nonagenarian, former U.S. Senator, Cornelius Cole who retired to the area. He no sooner passed on than Colegrove was stricken from the record and it became the southern part of Hollywood proper. Everything west of Hollywood all the way to Beverly Hills was once known as Sherman, after that respected pioneer of local mass transit, General Moses H. Sherman. Respected or not, Sherman was swallowed up and emerged as West Hollywood.

The Hollywood name had so much punch that Culver City tried to co-opt it since, as that locality pointed out, with MGM and Ince and Selznick International and Hal Roach, it had just as much right to being called the movie capital of the world as did H*******d. Eventually, the civic animosity rose to the point where the two Chambers of Commerce had to get together and formally bury the axe, much to the delight of local newspaper readers.

Los Angeles frequently pointed out that there was no Hollywood, that it had long ago disincorporated, and was now only a neighborhood. "Friends," long-time *Times* columnist Lee Shippey wrote, "Hollywood is the bunk. There's no such place—it is a state of mind. Culver City and Burbank and Malibu Beach are all 'Hollywood' and yet none of them is Hollywood. There is a section of Los Angeles which is called Hollywood (just as there are sections of Paris which are called Passy and Montmartre) and in the beginning the motion picture studios were in it. There was beautiful country all around them . . . and the companies had only to go a few blocks to find the scenes they needed."

But, said Lee Shippey, those days were long gone, Hollywood's beauty with them. Movies were made elsewhere, and "You may find more Hollywood atmosphere at Palm Springs or Lake Arrowhead. Do not look for 'Hollywood' in Hollywood. You're more likely to find it in Beverly Hills," Shippey concluded. Which was right in fact and wrong in the public imagination.

Shippey's wasn't the only attack. In 1937, an irate L.A. city councilman tried to stop the onslaught of creeping Hollywoodism by getting a resolution passed officially defining its limits: Hoover and Riverside Drive on the east; Mulhol-

land Drive on the north; Doheny on the west; and Melrose Avenue on the south. The cocktail parties, the colorful soirées, the glittering premières, the tinsel of Hollywood hemmed in by nothing Melrose Avenue? No one was impressed.

What galled L.A. was that Hollywood was a dull place even by Southern California's somnambulistic standards. The shops shuttered by nine. In fact, it was generally conceded that a cannonball could be fired from the intersection of Hollywood and Vine toward La Brea without endangering human life or limb.

Things started moving when master movie showman Sid Grauman opened his architecturally oddball Egyptian Theater in 1926 followed, two years later, by his masterpiece, the most glorious movie palace of them all, Grauman's Chinese. They joined hotels like the Knickerbocker and the stately old Hollywood Hotel, where the sight of Rudolph Valentino strolling through the lobby caused women to faint. There were eateries like Cafe Montmartre, with its private upstairs dining rooms, and the Armstrong and Carleton Cafe, popular with the film set. Al Levy, Los Angeles' most famous restaurateur, moved to Hollywood in the 1930s and Mike Lyman's Grill was down the street. Crowds jammed the Gotham Delicatessen and dens like the Cafe Morocco, where vintage 1928 champagne was $8.50 a bottle, pre-Prohibition bourbon 50¢ a shot and Meukow's N.P.U. grande fine champagne cognac (1848) was $1.50 a snifter. For the less refined of palate, there was the ever-popular C.C. Brown's where a generous hot fudge sundae was available for 35¢, whipped cream and nuts included.

The most famous Hollywood gathering spot was the Brown Derby. The original Brown Derby, the one in the shape of a hat, was still doing good business down on Wilshire, across from the Ambassador Hotel. But the Hollywood branch, more simple, elegant inside, was where the stars went. Owner Bob Cobb was one of the few, along with Dave Chasen of Chasen's or Mike Romanoff of Romanoff's, who could genuinely lay claim to the title of restaurateur to the

Left. One of Hollywood's most familiar landmarks under construction, NBC's Sunset and Vine studios. When it opened, this corner was the radio center of the world.

Right. CBS' Vine Street Studios, ca the mid1930s.

stars. In fact, Bob Cobb literally owned the Hollywood Stars — Pacific Coast League baseball team, that is.

It was the success of the Derby, with the crowds of tourists it generated, which was credited with giving the nearby intersection of Hollywood and Vine its glittering international reputation. In 1919–1920, the four corner lots at Hollywood and Vine could have been purchased for around $30,000. Ten years later, they were worth close to $8,000,000.

In 1919, the population of Hollywood had been 35,000 living among pepper and eucalyptus trees off dirt roads. By the mid-1920s, the population had risen to 150,000 and the dirt roads had disappeared. There were now sixteen grade schools, two junior and two senior high schools, thirty-nine churches, thirty-three banks, and eighteen hotels with a total of 1,500 rooms. Hollywood Boulevard between Argyle and La Brea was referred to as "skyscraper mile" for the imposing height of the new buildings. However, judgments like skyscraper are relative. It was only in 1925 that the first building exceeding 150 feet was approved.

Hollywood Boulevard gradually became the Broadway of the West. By the end of the 1920s almost 50,000 theatergoers could be accommodated in the community's theaters. The Music

Box, El Capitan and Pot Boiler Art Theater offered legitimate theater. In January of 1927, two major new legitimate theaters opened: the Vine Street with *An American Tragedy* and the Hollywood Playhouse with *Alias the Deacon*. In the mid-1930s, the Vine Street was converted into the CBS Radio Theater and it was from there that Hollywood came calling on the Lux Radio Theater. Despite the Depression, theatrical producer Henry Duffy, who opened the El Capitan in 1926, ran ten consecutive years without a dark night owing to lack of audience. It was an achievement he claimed no other theater in the country could equal.

The most famous Hollywood theater was the Hollywood Bowl. It was a creation of the old Hollywood and had practically nothing to do with the movies. The Bowl site was picked out in 1919 by a community group. In 1921, the site was used for Easter Sunrise services, inaugurating a tradition. Music was provided by the then recently created Los Angeles Philharmonic, with conductor Walter Rothwell on the podium. But when the money had been raised and the Bowl laid out, Rothwell declined the honor of leading the first summer outdoor concerts. He felt that music outside was either too unrefined or too cold or both. So the honor of being the first conductor went to bearded, roly-poly Alfred Hertz, San

Left. Hollywood as people saw it in the mid1930s, when the sky was nearly always clear and what you saw was a sea of bungalows.

Right. The view which thrilled every tourist in Hollywood—the bright carpet of the stars which was Hollywood Boulevard. In the foreground, famous Grauman's Chinese Theatre, and the middle ground, the famous Hollywood Hotel, in the late 1930s.

Francisco's maestro. The Bowl was off and running.

Immediately prior to the start of the second season, the city announced that it intended digging up Highland Avenue which ran past the Bowl. It was well commented upon how the city inevitably waited until the start of the tourist season before deciding to cripple traffic with destructive reconstruction. The city didn't reckon with the hard-headed civic mindedness of Hollywood and, on the day work was scheduled to begin, engineers arrived only to find two grandmotherly ladies, Bowl mover-groovers, seated in rocking chairs, blocking the path of progress. The resulting publicity was too much for the engineers and they were forced to withdraw. So began another, long-standing civic tradition, one that dictated that no one makes noise in or around the Hollywood Bowl during the concert season.

The Bowl was one of Hollywood's most enduring attractions. It was mesmerizing. Why? Classical music was something that for most people happened in the stuffy confines of ornate, imposing buildings. Here was classical music, well, semiclassical, outside, all bright and cheery. There was something democratic, something accessible about it. The Hollywood Bowl summarized what was attractive about Los Angeles.

The 1920s were big years for Hollywood and the movies. The film industry made more money in this decade than it would in what was generally considered to be the Golden Age, the 1930s. Audiences were huge, production costs, including salaries, low. Before long, the film industry was collecting somewhere around $1 billion each year at the box office in the United States alone. Clearly it was one of the biggest industries in Los Angeles even if downtown preferred to overlook it. In Hollywood, where a quarter of the population at least was working directly for the movies, the industry paid out a weekly payroll of $2 million. Which definitely encouraged merchants to stay up past nine at night.

One spark plug of Hollywood commerce was unique. Otto K. Oleson modestly claimed to having lit up the world. It was indeed his bright idea to convert the humble searchlight into a tool of modern publicity. He bought, so the story goes, a war-surplus carbon arc lamp off a battleship and mounted it on wheels, thereby creating a dazzling, sky-sweeping beam of light which, when flashed across the basin, proved an irresistible attraction. Before long, no debut of any kind, from the latest feature film to the opening of a dry cleaner, was complete without Otto K. and his light brigade.

Above. An Otto K. Oleson special: massed searchlights at the Hollywood Bowl, in the mid 1930s.

Below. The Hollywood Bowl undergoes construction, 1926.

So famous did Oleson become that Los Angeles' most famous, and most sophisticated, cabaret theater felt called upon to serve him up. The Yale Puppeteers—Forman Brown, Harry Burnett, and Richard Brandon—in the early '30s ran a small theater which graced renovated Olvera Street. Their patented blend of humor and satire, in song and puppet sketches, delighted all right-thinking Los Angeles. One of their vehicles was a slightly reworked Noah's Ark. In the Yale version, the Ark lands not on Ararat but, just like the rest of the world, in Los Angeles. Where, naturally, it was met by Otto K. Oleson, as the Puppeteers sang:

Let there be light says Otto K. Oleson,
And we flood the heavens with our beams.
Let there be light says Otto K. Oleson,
And the firmament gleams.
The stars and planets that twinkle down—
To extinguish 'em is our motto.
Though God lights the skies over every other
   town,
In Hollywood it's done by Otto!
Let there be light says Otto K. Oleson—
Venus and Mars, go hide yourselves away!
Our emancipator, our illuminator, Otto K!
Mrs. Throttlebottom has a hot dog stand—
She wants it to open in a manner grand.
So she calls on Otto and his trusty wights,
And we dash right over with our big arc lights.
We swing 'em low, and we swing 'em high—
We swing 'em all over the big blue sky—
Till Jupiter and Saturn just resign,
For this is Mrs. Throttlebottom's night to shine.
If you've got a drive-in or a beauty shop,
Or a filling station where you make one stop,
Or a barber college, or a burlesque show,
Or a Turkish bath in a bungalow,
Or an ice cream parlor, or a coffee pot,
Or a delicatessen, or a used car lot,
Or a mortuary or a cabaret,
We'll dim the glimmer of the Milky Way.
Let there be light says Otto K. Oleson . . .*

* *Otto K. Oleson*, words and music by Forman Brown, ASCAP. Used with gratitude and admiration for genius.

Otto K. Oleson's minions ready to sail forth and shed light. And sound.

Oleson was, for years, the lighting adviser behind the spectacular shows staged outdoors at the Hollywood Bowl and the nearby Pilgrimage Theater. And it was Otto K. who dreamed up the idea of changing the name of Hollywood Boulevard each holiday season to Santa Claus Lane and staging a parade. Oleson provided the elaborate decorations which graced the boulevard's lamp-posts, and even the float upon which Santa himself rode into town. All his public relations genius Oleson invested in Hollywood, much to the disgust, and admiration, of downtown Los Angeles.

There were other ways in which Hollywood influenced Los Angeles, much to L.A.'s displeasure. The movies had an impact on clothing styles, the most famous example being when Clark Gable bared his chest in *It Happened One Night* and the men's undershirt industry went into a nose dive. Scottish plaids were a fad after Hepburn in *Mary, Queen of Scots,* sailor collars after Ginger Rogers in *Follow the Fleet,* and mantillas were big after Loretta Young in *Ramona.* But, truth to tell, Los Angeles was never outrageously stylish when it came to clothing, so what impact the movies had was inevitably filtered through Paris and New York. But

Los Angeles *was* impressed with what it saw on the streets. When Marlene Dietrich was seen wearing male attire, it was startling news which was featured in the day's newspapers. FILM QUEEN IN MEN'S CLOTHES STARTLES CITY, the *Daily News* headlined. The secret came out: Garbo was known to wear corduroy trousers during informal walks in the Bel-Air hills, as did Billy Dove and Lily Damita. But Dietrich took it one step further, styling her clothes after Maurice Chevalier. She wore a suit, shirt and tie, flat-heeled brogues and a soft felt hat. Men with young sisters were urged to hide their suits lest "sister borrow it to keep step." Dietrich showed up once in masculine attire at the Hollywood Brown Derby. Comedians Wheeler and Woolsey were among the diners startled into silence when Dietrich made her entrance. They immediately got up, crossed the street to nearby Bullock's Department Store, and returned to parade through the restaurant attired in drag.

This Is Hollywood

From towering hills on which I stood
I said, "So this is Hollywood!"
Beneath were churches, homes and parks,
Where children played and meadow larks
Sang happy lays. There to my right
The Bowl of Hollywood in sight,
Where music's banners to the wind
Float free and beckon all mankind.
And down a green, secluded street
I saw a league where women meet.
A hundred I looked into
And there found hearts and souls as true
As e'er abide in this old world,
And then this shout of joy I hurled:
"Can this place, then, be Hollywood?
I see no evil, only good."
   — Palmer, *History of Hollywood*

Worse yet was the avalanche of gossip about Hollywood. Film people supposedly lived fast and loose. As libertine as Hollywood was reported to be, that was as conservative as Los

Angeles fancied itself. Neither was true. Numerous scandals erupted over the years which cast the socially prominent downtown in featured roles. And generations of tourists and immigrants were aghast to learn that, socially, Hollywood was an overgrown village with few nightclubs and little taste for staying up late. Still, the exceptions proved the rule.

The year 1922 was a bad one for Hollywood. In January, William Desmond Taylor, a film director with a murky past and murkier taste in what he did with women, was found shot dead. The murder darkened the careers of two of his supposed paramours, Mabel Normand, who later was involved with narcotics, and Mary Miles Minter. The case was never solved.

Then, in December, Los Angeles learned that handsome leading man Wallace Reid was dying of complications stemming from a narcotics habit. The story was lurid front page news, even in the staid *Times* which normally never printed a name below cabinet rank on its front page. The *Times* was in a difficult position. The paper could hardly level the salvo it wished for, whatever it thought of the film business, those with power in it did have friends downtown. Reid's habit was laid to drugs he'd taken after an accident suffered while shooting. And to the Hollywood lifestyle. According to his wife: "Many people came here [Reid's home] uninvited and remained for hours. They stayed until the liquor was gone. Some of them stole whiskey by the quart. When Wally recovers," she added, "we are going to sell this house and build a new one in some remote spot." Reid never did recover. He died in January of 1923. Almost as prominent as the report of his death was the cautionary tale headlined: REID WANTED TO DIRECT. In it, Reid was quoted as having said that he "never wanted to be an actor." His real ambition was to be a director, a job with some respectability. He had sworn that what had happened to his father would never happen to him. "My father could have been a great playwright but they wouldn't let him. Some of the box office boys got him to write a lurid 'mellerdramer' and it made a hit. After that they

would never take anything else from him." Success is hard to take.

The death of Taylor and Reid and an earlier even more lurid affair involving Fatty Arbuckle, prompted the movie industry to bring in Will Hays as its self-appointed censor.

The *Times* took advantage of all the publicity to get off a shot not at Hollywood but at its great rival, Hearst's *Examiner*. The *Times* revealed that, while the *Examiner* was taking a conciliatory line toward Hollywood, Hearst's *Chicago American* was doing anything but. The Chicago paper blasted Hollywood for its "dance of death. . . . Gangs of drug smugglers and bootleggers have grown rich on the depravities of Hollywood." Shame, shame.

From the very first, old-line, blue-blooded Los Angeles turned up its pedigreed nose at Hollywood and everyone connected with it. From the studio executives and stars on down, few were accepted into polite society. Exceptions were Mary Pickford and Douglas Fairbanks but even Mary suffered a social setback after their divorce. No others needed apply, despite the fact that a liaison had connected high society with Charlie Chaplin and Tom Mix among others in charitable work as early as the First World War. The Southwest Blue Book, unchallenged arbiter of local society, acted as if Hollywood didn't exist. "Oh, I admire picture people most sincerely," said Blue Book editor Leonora King Berry condescendingly, "but for thirty-six years the Southwest Blue Book has had a definite character — strictly society. So few of the screen people are society in that sense. If I included them it would just be a different book altogether." Oh.

A few had made it. Theda Bara, of all people, had snuck in, as Mrs. Charles Brabin. "Perhaps I'm for contrast," she said. "And then, I sinned only on the screen." Mrs. Elisabeth Fraser Lloyd was in, but her son Harold was barred. Both Cecil B. and William De Mille were in. Ramon Navarro was in, but got dropped. John Wayne was in, but only so long as he was married to Josephine Saenz, the daughter of a diplomat.

When that marriage ended in divorce, so did the Duke's tenure in the Book. Judge Bernard Douras and his daughter Reine Davies were included, but not his daughter Marion. Rosamond Pinchot, scion of one of Pennsylvania's most respected families, niece of progressive Governor Gifford Pinchot was unceremoniously dropped when she declared herself a movie actress. Mayer, Lasky, and Schenck were names consistently omitted: whatever their authority in movies, they were also Jews, and that counted for three strikes. Mr. and Mrs. Sam Goldwyn were in the social diaspora but her sister, Constance Howard, was an insider. Everybody else, from the Barrymores to Will Rogers, was out.

Occasionally, the deep-seated animosity between social Los Angeles and Hollywood broke out into the open. Ruben Schmidt, a speaker for the Chamber of Commerce, was denied permission to address an audience attending a screening of the film *Arizona* at the Philharmonic because, according to the film's exhibitor, the Chamber of Commerce had never done anything for the motion picture industry except "put 'made in Los Angeles' on films." Two producers, both millionaires, were asked to resign from the Los Angeles Country Club because of their industry affiliation. Two girls had the door of an apartment they wanted to rent slammed in their faces because the landlady found out they were in pictures. According to a report published in 1920, "There are many places, especially out Hollywood way, where there are signs, 'No peddlers, agents, dogs or movie actors allowed.'"

Another form of local discrimination was slightly more subtle. In the early days of the movies, producers resisted paying their actors and actresses anything beyond a pourboire. The emergence of the star system changed that and executives flip-flopped, realizing there was publicity hay to be made from the fact they were paying their stars such fabulous figures. "First Million-Dollar Deal Signed — Harry Langdon and First National," the *Daily News* trumpeted in 1925. "Although the exact amount of the contract was not announced, it's known that it represents a real fortune, where fortunes begin at a large figure." People would go to movies to see what was worth one million dollars about Harry Langdon. The effect this had locally was disastrous as far as everybody else in movies was concerned. Film folks were constantly being overcharged by grocers, doctors, lawyers and dentists. Why not? They made so much.

In the teens and early 1920s, actors and actresses lived fairly nondescript lives in Los Angeles. Their residences were usually modest but then a little went a long way when it came to housing in Los Angeles. The advent of the star system had one definite impact on the Los Angeles landscape. As money flowed into the business and more of it found its way into the hands of the stars, they began to live life more gloriously and with less thought of frugality. That included their housing. Moreover, the studios realized that, in addition to the sums they paid their stars, there was publicity mileage in the manner in which the stars lived. The bigger the better, the more romantic it made films. The stage was set when Doug Fairbanks met Mary Pickford and, in 1919, together they began the renovation, actually complete reconstruction, of a hunting lodge in the hills. What finally emerged was the grand estate of Pickfair, a residence fit for America's uncrowned king and queen, who were married the next year. It was the first, only the first, of what historian Charles Lockwood called the "dream palaces."

Once there was a first, everybody could measure their success in Hollywood. The building of estates both well-conceived and garish would be a local pastime for the next twenty years. Gloria Swanson redid the old King Gillette mansion in Beverly Hills, converting it into a royal residence with twenty-two rooms and five baths. Rudolph Valentino built his Falcon Lair high up Benedict Canyon. Harold Lloyd's Greenacres cost more than $2,000,000 and featured a golf course and a canoe pond and was the most majestic Hollywood estate ever constructed. William Randolph Hearst built paramour Marion Davies an immense beachfront home by the

Luxury homes taking root in the
Hollywood Hills, along Catalina
Avenue, in 1930. Before long, these
and thousands like them would
disappear beneath a shield of lush
California vegetation.

Roosevelt Highway in Santa Monica, which became the site of legendary parties. Eventually, the stars migrated out of downtown and the better residential districts around the mid-Wilshire district and Hancock Park, working their way into the foothills of the Los Feliz district, and west, to the flatlands of Beverly Hills north of Santa Monica Boulevard and into the hills off Benedict and Coldwater canyons, and thence to Bel-Air. Doug and Mary could horseback ride from Pickfair to the ocean, but they also kept a beach "cottage," small only in the gargantuan Hollywood sense, which started the trend of stars having a second home at Santa Monica or, later, at Malibu.

When the idea first occurred to a tourist to go and see one of these houses unannounced is lost in history. But, it was evident to entrepreneurs early on what the public wanted to do while in Los Angeles, as witness this from the *Los Angeles Daily News* in May, 1924:

"HEIGH-HO! FILM STARS' ADDRESSES TO GO ON SALE

Loud wails from the aristocracy of Hollywood motion picture circles may soon be heard. According to Don Belding, disabled veteran being rehabilitated by the Lord and Thomas Advertising Agency, he has compiled a volume containing the addresses of sixty-five of the most prominent picture stars residing in the studio section of the city.

This pamphlet, Belding says, will go on sale today on downtown newsstands. In addition to the addresses, Belding says explicit directions showing how to reach the home of each of the sixty-five will be afforded.

As a consequence, several picture stars last night were reported preparing to seek other abodes, or thinking of locking the doors and entering their residences by means of an underground tunnel system.

They declare enthusiastic admirers are entirely to their liking, but object to having their residences made known generally lest the 'fans' stage demonstrations at any or all hours before their gates."

Which is exactly what the fans did do. By the early 1930s, addresses of the stars' homes were routinely included in official tourist bureau publications, and maps were offered for sale by roadside vendors around the city. The streets around some homes had to be widened to accommodate the crowds.

If a tourist missed his or her favorite star at home, there was one place they were sure to be, the studio. The studios were the Meccas for Hollywood-bound pilgrims. But between the crowds and the objects of their affection stood the stalwart gate guard. Every studio had one and his duty was to keep the unauthorized out.

The gate guards had heard it all and seen it all. Popular lines fed to these lions included the tourist being the husband/wife of someone inside, having urgent, private business or being a theatrical exhibitor or newspaperman. "Now naturally," said one guard, "the studio wants to treat all theater owners cordially, but they come here by the thousands and they can't all be exhibitors! And the newspapermen, Lord! There can't be more than a few thousand of 'em in Los Angeles and environs, but it seems like they come here by the hundred thousand."

The tourists who did get beyond the gates were inevitably disappointed by what they saw inside. There was something disillusioning about walking through a living room set complete in every detail and emerging on to a bare stage. "Most of them hate the idea of the beautiful setting being torn down after each picture," a guard remarked. "How are we ever to tell what's real and what isn't in pictures?" implored a visitor.

Tourists were largely barred from the studios because there was serious work going on inside and they'd get in the way. But there were other more obscure reasons. For instance, one tourist who got a tour had a Kodak and snapped away. He sold his photos to a producer who made a copy of the film the tourist had seen in production and got it to the theaters before the major studio's product.

But when a tourist did crack the gates, there was one place he or she was sure to head: the

Central Casting, 1923. The cards on the desk contain the names of 10,000 hopefuls waiting by their phones in the hope of a day's work as an extra. The man at the rear in the bow tie booked juveniles. Rose, the switchboard operator, phoned the lucky ones.

studio cafeteria. These were legendary not for their food, but for the chance to grab a peek of a star feeding his or her face. Paramount's cafeteria was a huge room, divided by a partition. MGM's had a porch which featured the fabled director's table. Fox's was elegant, the room decorated with colorful murals. Warner's had a private green room for the stars while Universal had a general cafeteria open to the public.

Having sampled the fare at one of the studios, the tourist was now trapped. There is no count of the thousands, perhaps millions, who were either lured out West by the hoped of making it in the movies or who, once they visited, decided they could never leave. It was generally thought that, in the 1920s, the percentage of attractive young women on the streets had risen dramatically and that the movies were responsible. Or were to blame depending on your point of view.

Newcomers were warned to avoid con men who promised, for a fee, to get a would-be star a set of publicity photos, an appointment with a casting director or enrolled in a "school" which could teach the secrets of screen success. One stop all hopefuls made was at Central Casting, a nondescript building on Hollywood Boulevard, where the hopefuls filled out cards listing all their skills. The cards were filed by type, and, maybe, some morning, the phone would ring with a job, a day's work, paying between $5 and $15.

Central Casting had developed in the mid-1920s. In the early days, each studio had an interview yard out-of-doors called a "bullpen" where, regardless of weather, would-be stars lined up each morning. They eagerly awaited the morning a casting director might appear and, throwing a fish eye over those assembled, would shout out "Hey, you!" The casting director at MGM once remarked that he figured the odds against anyone actually getting in the movies in any meaningful way to be 5,000–1. And becoming a star? Maybe 25,000–1. Does that sound too generous?

Of course, lightning could always strike and the hopefuls lived for the unexpected. The most thunderous burst must have been in the 1930s when, with China and Japan at war, films like *Roar of the Dragon, War Correspondent,* and *Shanghai Express* suddenly became very popular. It became difficult to get good service in a downtown chop suey joint: everybody in Chinatown was working as an extra in the movies. As part of a crowd, extras got $7.50 a day and, if they were required to speak, even in Chinese, $10–$15. It was estimated Los Angeles' Chinese community was putting in 30,000 days' work a year, which meant a cash infusion of between $200,000 and $250,000.

That's the way it was in topsy-turvy Hollywood. War was good for business.

In the middle of the 30's, Culver City waged war on Hollywood. The community named after realtor Harry Culver insisted it should be considered the center of filmdom. After all, within its boundaries were MGM with "more stars than there are in the heavens," Hal Roach, Selznick International and more. It was a well-publicized tiff good for miles of publicity up to and including the moment the two chambers of commerce got together to bury the hatchet. One minor irony clouded Culver City's claim. The town's most famous resident, MGM's world-renowned Leo the Lion whose roar opened every studio product, was no resident at all, but rather lived in the faraway town of El Monte, at Gay's Lion Farm. And Gay's, the most curious of the many different institutions that supplied animal actors, was its own chapter in the entertainment history of Southern California.

El Monte is one of the oldest settlements in Los Angeles county: as far as being pure Anglo, it's the oldest. During the Civil War, the word "union" wasn't mentioned on the streets of what the locals called Monte and the Confederate flag flew at the announcement of a Rebel victory. By the 1920s, the Civil War had passed, but El Monte still attracted Southerners. Its most famous resident but one was the Reverend Robert "Fighting Bob" Shuler, pastor at Los Angeles' prestigious Trinity Methodist Church South, a Baptist who flayed away at sin and excess in the city but who, when sundown came, retreated to the peace and insularity of El Monte.

But the town's most famous resident was a man named Charles Gay and he had nothing at all to do with either the South or with religion. His stock in trade was raising lions.

In 1919, Gay opened up Gay's Lion Farm, just east of downtown on Valley Boulevard. For the next twenty-four years, the farm was open to the public Tuesdays through Sundays, from 10:00 a.m. to 5:00 p.m., except for rainy days.

Gay, born in Paris, had learned his English in London, where he'd become associated with the wild animal dealer, W. Simson Cross. Gay became fascinated with lions. "The lion is vulgarly known as the king of beasts," he said. "He is far from it. Many animals surpass him in intelligence. He is practically untameable and always treacherous. But he is courageous and majestic."

Gay had learned to tame lions from the Englishman, Fred C. Bostock. Then Gay had joined a circus which, all the romance aside, he hated. Finding himself in California, he quit his job and looked around for a new occupation. It so happened that, at about the same time, events were occurring in India which provided him with a new career. Lions there were wreaking havoc upon the villages and so the English authorities put a bounty on lions. That, plus the well-known appetite of English gentlemen for a good lion hunt, had made it cheaper to shoot the beasts than trap and export them. Gay went into business raising lions for the markets outside of India which could no longer get lions.

Beginning with three lions, two females and a male, Gay took to raising the animals. The first few years were difficult. Gay succeeded in training two lions for work in the movies. Slats and Numa became famous, and Gay charged $100 a day for them when they were working. The rest

Charles Gay and his trained lions.

Above. Charles Gay astride one of his favorite (and tame) lions, Pluto.

Below. Approaching Gay's Lion Farm in El Monte. On Monday nights, the big cats didn't get fed and then you didn't need a sign, you could hear them roaring for miles.

of the time they resided at the Farm where an endless line of tourists crowded by a real taste of the jungle, right in El Monte. As Gay's advertised: "To visit the great Southwest and not see Gay's Lion Farm is like going to Egypt and not seeing pyramids."

Gay's wasn't the only animal installation in Southern California. There were, at various times, dozens more. Pigeons roosted by the thousands at a special farm in the San Fernando Valley until the raging waters of the Los Angeles River in flood drowned the feathered creatures. The Los Angeles Ostrich Farm near Lincoln Park offered all any tourist could want to know about this odd-ball bird. The most famous ostrich farm, Cawston's in South Pasadena, folded in the '20s no longer able to make ends meet after the fad of ostrich feathers in lady's hats passed away. The California Alligator Farm on Mission Road was another perennial favorite.

Most animal farms, like Gay's, were created to serve the motion picture industry. The granddaddy was the Selig Zoo also on Mission Road which was so big and elaborate that most tourists and some residents assumed it was the city zoo. It contained 700 species of animals and birds, all available for rent: elephants at $200 a day, monkeys between $25 and $50. The residents most people wanted to see were the stars. Mary, a chimpanzee famous in films Selig produced, was insured for $100,000. Dogs like Strongheart and Teddy, a Great Dane and comedy star, were closely tended. Cameo, another canine luminary, made $200 a week and, since she had weak eyes and the lights used in early film-making were so strong, she wore specially tinted glasses. Early in the days of Hollywood, it was a dog's life.

Chinatown was known for its
gambling dens, which, as often as not,
were left unmolested by the police. In
this case, the fix must not have been
in and the joint was raided, 1938.

8

CHINATOWN: THE MYSTERIOUS EAST MEETS THE EQUALLY MYSTERIOUS WEST

Los Angeles' Chinatown might not have been as large as San Francisco's but, as far as Occidental Los Angeles was concerned, it was every bit as mysterious and imposing. The dimly lit spider's web of narrow streets and alleys, teeming with pig-tailed Orientals pursuing unfathomable routines, seemed a million miles away from the other, sun-drenched Los Angeles. White folks went to Chinatown for one of two reasons: to eat, and everything else, and everything else, likely as not, was illegal everywhere else.

Chinatown, to the south and east of the downtown Plaza, had always been a center of prostitution. Ladies of every ethnic description were available. Los Angeles was, as well, a center for the importation of drugs, chiefly opium. Around the turn of the century, it was estimated there were 100 opium dens open for business. Restrictions on the use of the drug came in the first decade of the new century. A tax of $7.50 a pound was applied which, it was thought, was so stiff it would smother the trade. Then, in 1912, opium was outlawed. Underground the price shot up to $105 a pound. That didn't stop about

10,000 tins a year from being imported, each tin weighing half a pound and costing $60 delivered to the corner of Los Angeles and Commercial streets. Dope smoking was a rich man's preoccupation for a habit cost, in the 1930s, about $1.50 a day. It wasn't until the end of the decade that events and the Feds conspired to break the back of the opium trade.

Chinatown and the Chinese rarely came to public attention unless they ran afoul of the law. Tong wars were one exotic pastime the newspapers gleefully recounted. The tongs, fraternal organizations that assumed the dimensions of a gang, were strictly an American innovation and had only a superficial relationship to behavior in China. Their shadowy beginnings were in the California of the 1870s, and they grew until, by the 1920s, they were a prominent feature of Chinatown life, organizations men of prominence either joined or at least tacitly acknowledged.

The two main Los Angeles tongs were the Bing Kong, who had their origins in the Freemasons and offices on Apablasa Street, and the Hop Sing, quartered in the two-story, crumbling old Lugo home which faced the Plaza. Relations between the two were calm until 1908 when war broke out over a woman a member of one tong "sold" to a member of the other. She turned out to have tuberculosis which made her damaged goods, a deficit the seller refused to acknowledge. The matter was taken to the streets and half a dozen died. Two Hop Sings died at the intersection of Los Angeles and Alameda streets of what one member of the LAPD picturesquely referred to as "internal exposure."

In 1910, Wong Fong, the "mayor" of Los Angeles' Chinatown and a prominent Bing Kong was shot to death in San Francisco. For the next decade, the Hop Sings were the dominant force. In the early 1920s yet another war broke out. Three members of the Bing Kong were gunned down on Alameda as they left a fan-tan game. Patrolman H. F. Glaze of the Chinatown Squad was only half a block away when the shooting broke out. He gave chase but lost the gunmen around Alameda and Macy. "The tragedy was enacted when the night life of Chinatown was at its zenith," a newspaper remarked cynically. "Officers stood on every corner. Dark figures were shuffling through the narrow streets. But when the six shots echoed through Chinatown, there was a rapid scramble for secret doorways and alleyways, and Chinatown was as if deserted."

Retribution came two months later, during Chinese New Year. Bing Kongs killed two Hop Sings and wounded a third. Hop Sing member Lem Gooey Fong was dozing behind the counter of his store on Marchessault when gunmen entered and opened fire. Soo Ho Long was playing dominos on Apablasa when assailants fingered him. At the same time, four more Bing Kongs were being shot to death in San Francisco.

Sporadic violence flared through the decade until in the late 1920s Police Chief James Edgar Davis announced: "It is time that these campaigns of murder among the Chinese stop." He was largely successful. Open warfare, and later the tongs themselves, faded from the scene.

The instrument of Davis' anger was the Chinatown Detail, noted for its bellicosity and lack of subtlety. It was not for nothing that its one-time leader, Dick Steckel, got the name "Strongarm Dick" while on duty downtown.

Gambling was an unmistakable part of Chinatown life and its forms were many and varied. The lottery was ever popular and proved interesting to whites as well who adopted it under the name of keno. Mah jong, too, was passed on to the majority. Visitors to Chinatown were struck by the clatter of tiles that could be heard on every street. Even more exotic were games like pai gow, a form of dominos, or tse-far, a game that involved discovering the identity of a hidden tile through the answering of a riddle.

Gambling was so much an attraction that it was generally believed the Chinatown Detail protected it. In the mid-1930s, somebody who obviously possessed an insider's knowledge circulated among officials and the newspapers a letter giving in detail the workings of the fix. Supposedly more than $400,000 a year was passing into official hands. Paying off the cops wasn't the only step operators were willing to take to insure their profitability. When the fates were running against patrons and they were going elsewhere, an owner would paint or redecorate, a measure guaranteed to even things out. When luck was running the other way and the house was getting hit, managers would immediately stage a free public feast and offer every sort of sweet as a way of propitiating evil spirits.

For the Chinese, Chinatown was a city within a city offering all the services they required, from a theater (the Joke Wah Ming Company from Hong Kong took up residence on Court Street in the 1920s) to what was reputed to be the only Chinese blacksmith in the country. There was a joss house, a temple at Marchessault and Juan Streets, and, not far away, the vegetable market. This open-air wholesale market with its rickety wood stands was vitally important to the life of the community. Once, more than 600 Chinese were employed in the door-to-door vending of fresh vegetables around Los Angeles. There was a Chinese Museum School, and modern apartments, the Sun Way, on Apablasa.

chow mein came fried either Chicago or Canton style, and visitors were introduced to fried won ton, a specialty described as "Chinese raviolis with pickled sauce."

After such a dinner, a tourist was fortified for a stroll around Chinatown. If he made his way to the intersection of North Alameda and Marchessault streets, he was at the center of things. It would be busy regardless of the hour. The houses he saw, adobe and brick, were among the oldest in the city. The Chinese had added wooden balconies, often elaborately carved. From them dangled brightly colored banners inscribed with Chinese characters, the emblems of the tongs.

Along Marchessault were the grocery stores. Yee Sing Chong was one, recognizable by its brown and white striped awning. Inside, the large floor was covered with jars, tins and wooden boxes, their tops pried off to reveal exotic foods.

Further down Alameda was the famous poster wall on whose brick surface anybody could post a notice and the Chinese Chamber of Commerce attached a daily newspaper. For fifty years, the wall had served as the chief source of information for Chinatown.

If the visit was fortunate enough to have a native guide along, he would inevitably be taken to the North Main curio shop of Ah Tom, the unofficial mayor of Chinatown, amateur physician, counselor to all and representative of the Orient to the Occident. The curiosity was that Ah Tom was himself a white, his real name being Tom Gubbins. Gubbins had lived in Chinatown for years and reputedly spoke no less than thirty-five dialects.

Everything about Gubbins was, like Chinatown itself, mysterious and slightly exaggerated. He told different stories of his background at different moments. In one, he was the son of a German father and an Irish mother. Born in Shanghai, he was raised by a Chinese nurse or amah. In another version, his mother had long since died and his father had married his nurse.

The 5,000 Chinese of Chinatown looked to Ah Tom to run interference for them in face of

Illicit drugs, the spoils of a raid in Chinatown, ca the early 1920s.

Most of the life of Chinatown was hopelessly alien to Los Angeles but, at lunch or at dinner, East met West over a bowl of rice. Once Los Angeles discovered that Chinese food was not, as had been believed, poisonous, but good and cheap, the rush was on. The chop suey joints were inevitably located on the second story of Chinatown's frame and brick buildings because the rents were cheaper there.

Who cared (or knew) that chop suey wasn't Chinese at all, but American. At the Yee Hung Guey off Apablasa, patrons entered through the kitchen, the better to be enticed by the smells. Chicken chow mein was the specialty. At the Chinese Junk Cafe on North Main, four kinds of chow mein were offered, nine of chop suey and a special cocktail, the Chinese Junk, which cost 45 cents. At the Forbidden Palace, Li Hung Chong chop suey (pork, chicken, onion, water chestnuts, white mushrooms, bean sprouts, celery and bamboo shoots) was named for China's first minister to the United States. It cost 50 cents. The

Above. A waiter's eye view of one of Los Angeles' favorite pastimes, eating Chinese food, in New Chinatown, ca 1939.

Below. The interior of the Chinatown Chamber of Commerce, 1933.

the frequently frightening and certainly antithetic world around them. Gubbins literally had all Chinatown as his clients. In the late '20s and accelerating in the '30s, Japan and China were at war. War films with an Oriental background became a sub-genre of Hollywood and where there were movies, extras were needed. Gubbins agented Chinatown and everybody worked at $5.00 a day, including at times Loy Choy, at seventy-eight, the oldest resident of Chinatown.

Chinatown, alas, was a marked community. Since the turn of the century, eyes, covetous of the land it sat upon, had stared from nearby white downtown. The issue was brought to a head in the nearly two-decade-long argument over a new "union" railroad terminal for Los Angeles. Heretofore, the Santa Fe arrived at the La Grande Station on Santa Fe between First and Second Streets, a distinctive building with a Moorish dome. The Southern Pacific came into the Central Station, on Central between Fourth and Sixth.

The railroads weren't at all enthusiastic about the idea for a new terminal but Harry Chandler and the *Times* were. The ultimate decision, given that lineup, was never in doubt. In 1931, the California State Supreme Court cleared the last legal obstacles. Still, actual demolition didn't begin until the end of 1933. Notices were posted earlier that year telling the Chinese of their fate. Many residents could read neither the English nor the Chinese language versions. The old-timers held on, even after power and water had been turned off and the process of removing the sidewalks had begun. It wasn't until the wrecking crews started work on the buildings that the last reluctant residents left. The first victim of urban renewal was the two-story Bong Hing merchandise store at the corner of Apablasa and Juan, which in recent years had housed a school.

When it became obvious the Chinese were going to be forced to move the question arose: to where? There was no lack of schemes. "Every American who has a Chinese acquaintance," remarked community leader Peter Soo Hoo,

A dragon parade in celebration of the opening of the development, China City. The festivities didn't last long. China City burned down not long after it opened, in 1938.

"thought he had a deal cooked up. Every Chinese who has an American friend thought likewise." Soo Hoo's plan was to move the community a few blocks north and east, to a new location where the land would be owned, for the first time, by the Chinese themselves.

Society leader Christine Sterling had what she thought was a better idea. Her voice carried weight since it was she who had devised and brought to completion the Olvera Street project. She now proposed doing the same for (or was it to?) the Chinese. For them she intended China City. It was to be the idealization of everything people thought the Chinese needed and more. While the Chinese themselves appreciated the value of set decoration in attracting the public's attention, they thought China City, with its serpentine streets, twisting alleys, rickshaws and vendors selling food from carts a little too precious. "What do they want?" Mrs. Sterling huffed back, "A Chinese Westwood Village?"

Mrs. Sterling and the Chinese parted company. In June, 1938, her China City, centered at Ord and Spring, opened. The entrance was via an ornate gate dedicated, politically, to long-time *Times* columnist and old China hand Harry Carr. The main street was curvey Dragon Road off of which ran the Road of the Lotus to the Court of Four Seasons. The town hall was in the shape of a pirate junk. There was a candle shop, an all-too-obvious import from Olvera Street, and a restaurant where the chef was advertised as knowing 100 ways of fixing chicken.

If it all looked a little like it was out of some movie, it was. A set designer from Paramount had collaborated in the conception and C.B. De Mille had donated a lot of studio props and costumes associated with things Chinese. And, finally, scenes from *The Good Earth* were shot there.

This branch of the Celestial Empire was not long for the world. Six months after it opened, China City was devastated by fire. The conflagration was apparently set by a street vendor of pencils who hoped to reap a reward for reporting it. China City was eventually partly restored but, by then, it had lost its momentum in the race with Peter Soo Hoo's development, New Chinatown.

New Chinatown, a few blocks further east and north, also opened late in 1938. While all the touches were in Chinese style, the emphasis was on providing a modern, comfortable shopping area on land that the Chinese owned. New Chinatown proved a roaring success and for generations of Angelenos, both Oriental and Occidental, was the only Chinatown they had ever known.

Sister Aimee in the best of times, on the first anniversary of her Angelus Temple, 1924. The cake was made of biblical ingredients: flour (I Kings 4:22), butter (Judges 5:25), and sugar (Jer. 6:20). The cake fed 5,500 people and included 100 pounds of powdered sugar.

9

SISTER AIMEE SEMPLE MCPHERSON AND HER GUARANTEED, SURE-FIRE HEADLINES

The life of evangelist Aimee Semple McPherson, Sister they called her, was crowded with miracles. Born in Canada, she arrived, she was fond of recounting, in response to her mother's prayer for a girl baby to preach the gospel. However, another version of her story reveals that her parents were never thrilled by her addiction to Holy Roller Pentacostalism, they being good serving members of the Salvation Army, and even less enthusiastic when their daughter married a self-appointed preacher and took off for China. That trip ended in disaster with the death of Aimee's husband.

After returning, remarrying and eventually divorcing, Aimee took to the pulpit, organizing her own tent road show specializing in speaking in tongues and faith healing. Clearly Aimee had a flare. And appeal for, in those days before the First World War, she was effectively doing what had been man's work.

It was a nomadic life. In 1918, when her daughter was taken ill with influenza, Aimee had a vision. "These words were born in my heart," she said. "Don't cry, my child. Your little girl will live and not die. Moreover I will give you a bungalow for her in Los Angeles, California, where she can go to school." This was God talking and Aimee took His suggestion that life might be better in the Golden West.

She loaded her family and her gospel tent in a road-weary Olds emblazoned with the motto: "Jesus is Coming Soon—Get Ready," and, making 200 miles a day, drove west. Whether the motive to go to Los Angeles was divine or not, it was certainly inspired. Arriving, she wasn't the least disappointed not to find a brass band awaiting her. What she did notice was that there were a lot of tourists around, which must have reassured her, audiencewise. And, Aimee perceived, she had arrived not a moment too soon: "Here in this 'City of the Angels' where the power of the Spirit had so wonderfully fallen years previous, we learned that divers doctrinal differences had gotten the eyes of many off the Lord, and that there was a dearth in the land." The dearth would be no more, for Aimee, the most diverse of them all, had arrived.

She set up shop in Victoria Hall in down-

Left. Sister Aimee, accompanied by local Police Chief Murchinson and LAPD Detective Herman Cline in an ultimately futile effort to locate the cabin where she was held during her supposed abduction.

Right. Sister Aimee meets the press for the first time since her "abduction," at Douglas, Arizona, 1926.

town Los Angeles, still preaching in the Holy Roller style. She was successful and began to think of more permanent quarters. She was driving aimlessly about town one day, she recalled, when she chanced to enter the Echo Park district. She was immediately struck: "Why this is heaven on earth, the most beautiful spot for the house of the Lord that I have ever seen!" Sister took most such occurrences as divinely inspired. She was not disappointed when the vacant corner lot she set her eyes upon turned out to be the only parcel in the area not for sale. That simply meant that the Lord was saving it for her. Sure enough, upon inquiry, it turned out that the owner had decided, days previously, to sell.

With the land procured, Aimee set about designing a temple, Angelus Temple, in the shape of a pie wedge. Aimee's podium was to be at the apex. It opened January 1, 1923, and was an immediate success.

Aimee's appeal was based partly on her sex: she was not an unattractive woman and certainly personable and dynamic on the platform. And in preaching her Foursquare Gospel, she didn't ape the popular theme of the day: Hellfire and Brimstone awaited the sinner and all were sinners. Instead, Aimee confessed that she was much more interested in heaven than in hell, and in love as the way of getting up there. No bible-thumping, podium-pounding here.

But most of all, there was Sister's consum-

mate sense of theater. It manifested itself in her faith healing, a great show that Los Angeles never tired of watching. Soon, the Memory Room of the Temple was filling up with discarded crutches, wheelchairs and other sickroom supplies of those who received relief via Aimee. Other crasser aspects of Aimee's early evangelism were, like the crutches, laid aside. Now the rolling on the floor and talking in tongues was done in a separate, padded room in the Temple. Aimee had modified her act, becoming as properly middle class as Los Angeles itself.

Sister Aimee's greatest moments were her elaborately conceived and executed show sermons. Here was Sister dressed up as the Admiral of the Salvation Navy, complete with a gospel rowboat. The U.S. Navy objected to the cut of her uniform. Or Aimee as a traffic cop, warning the congregation "Stop! You're Breaking God's Law!" The inspiration for this sermon came from Aimee's arrest for speeding. Or Sister as George Washington, reviewing the troops at Valley Forge. She was a great one for costumes and one of the main pastimes of her world gospel tours was collecting native costumes which eventually would work their way into a sermon production back home.

Still, Aimee might have disappeared in clouds of obscurity had not her excitable nature presumably gotten the best of her. On the afternoon of May 18, 1926, Sister, accompanied by her secretary, went to the beach at Ocean Park for a swim. Somewhere around 4:00 p.m., the secretary glanced up toward the spot where Sister had been swimming. Now she was nowhere to be seen. She did not reappear nor was her body found.

The news that the popular evangelist had disappeared under mysterious circumstances set off a small carnival as thousands of the faithful and/or curious flocked to the beach to pray or to lend a hand in the efforts to find Aimee's remains. One diver, the Sheriff of Catalina, died as a result of the search. Days passed, and then weeks, with no clues. Aimee was presumed drowned. There were some ransom notes but

Sister Aimee in the worst of times, discussing her divorce with one of Los Angeles' most famous criminal lawyers, Jerry Giesler.

these were not taken seriously.

Memorial services for Aimee were held at Angelus Temple a month after her disappearance. Thousands bid her a fond adieu. And then, days later, another patented Aimee miracle occurred as the evangelist was found, having suddenly walked out of the desert around Agua Prieta, Mexico.

By way of explaining her absence, Aimee told of having been kidnapped by Steve and Rose, two ne'er-do-wells, who drove her to Mexico and kept her prisoner in a small desert shack. Unfortunately for Aimee, this shack could never be located, despite an intense search. Eyebrows were raised at that inconsistency and by others that surfaced. Her condition was remarkably good for one who supposedly had stumbled across a waterless desert. Her shoes hardly reflected the strain at all, in fact, they had grass stains, hard to come by in that part of Mexico. It was only the beginning of a long series of crazy angles to the case, which Aimee breezed her way past.

Sister's greatest antagonist in Los Angeles was the Reverend Fighting Bob Shuler. Shuler had long been outraged by Sister's many theological heresies and by her dependence upon the techniques of the theater for her success. A telling point, as far as Bob was concerned, was the fact that Aimee had "posed for more photographs than any other woman in America outside of show business." Coming into his own as a political power in Los Angeles, Shuler lectured to rallies called at his Trinity Methodist Church protesting official unwillingness to take action against Sister Aimee. When a grand jury was called to investigate, and dispersed, calling Aimee's story doubtful but concluding there wasn't evidence enough to prosecute her, Fighting Bob unleashed one of his most vitriolic attacks, embarrassing District Attorney Asa Keyes into further action.

If Aimee hadn't been kidnapped, what possible motive could she have had for such a bizarre stunt? The widely circulated story was that love was to blame. She was having an affair with a married man. The man was Kenneth Ormiston, a radio technician who had helped install one of the city's first radio stations at the offices of the *Los Angeles Times* and who, at the same time, had served as the paper's first radio editor. Later, he had set up Sister Aimee's station, KFSG (Kall Foursquare Gospel). One version of what was behind the caper was that Ormiston and Sister were, for the period that practically the entire city of Los Angeles was searching for them, ensconced in a cottage in romantic Carmel, California.

Charges in the kidnapping case were later dropped but, like an unattended wisdom tooth, they continued to cause trouble for Sister for years afterward. Her life thereafter never ran smoothly. There were hints of intrigue around the Temple and, eventually, they led to a falling-out between Aimee and her mother, Mother Kennedy as everyone knew her, as odd-ball in her way as Aimee was in hers. There was Aimee's spectacularly poor business sense which not only lost her money but caused her acute embarrassment. One project was the selling of cemetery lots near where Aimee herself promised to be buried. Buyers were offered the opportunity on that eventual glorious day to "Go Up with Aimee." There was a well-publicized, ill-conceived third marriage for Sister and a resulting divorce. Yet, through it all, Sister persevered.

There were good works along the way, such as the Temple's active food program during the Depression which fed thousands of the poor. But it was the spectacles the people came for and the actress Aimee the people wanted to see. One writer figured that, at the height of her celebrity, her name appeared on the front page of a Los Angeles newspaper on the average of three times a week. So much press guaranteed the Angelus Temple a place on every tourist's must-see list.

Venice, California, in its earliest and
most graceful incarnation. It wasn't
yet obvious that the water system that
fed the canals wasn't all that it should
have been, causing the channels to
have not only distinctive perspectives
but an olfactory accompaniment as
well. That came later. For the time
being, Venice was the surprising
creation of a fertile imagination.

10

HOW TO GO EVERYWHERE IN THE WORLD WITHOUT LEAVING HOME: TIJUANA, CATALINA AND VENICE

Tijuana,* Catalina, Venice: far distant suburbs which were as much a part of Los Angeles proper as City Hall. They lent themselves to one of Los Angeles' most powerful advertising claims: that you could go most anywhere in the world simply by visiting a Southern California whose environs were so variegated they suggested every other landscape around the planet. Tijuana was every exotic foreign city. Catalina every desert isle. Venice every beach resort.

Everybody knew what went on in Tijuana. It was a raucous bordertown where anything could happen and usually did. Depending on your point of view, it was a bastion of freedoms that Americans denied to themselves at home, or, as the *Times* put it, an "iniquitous eyesore."

Before the First World War, Sunny Jim Coffroth, also known as Pops, built the Tijuana Race Track since horse racing was illegal over the border in California. Coffroth, a fight promoter,

knew almost nothing about horse racing but he well appreciated the character of his compatriots. And Coffroth was smart enough to realize that to attract attention, he had to get good horses competing for big purses.

The track opened in 1916 and was a hit. The derby purse was $20,000 and the modestly named Coffroth Handicap offered $100,000, an amazing sum in its day. The track admitted 15,000 spectators and a good reason for its profitability was the hefty $5 admission charge, which kept it in the black with a minimum number of customers. Another reason for the track's success was that, shortly after it opened, Los Angeles went dry and, within a few years, the United States as a whole followed. There was no Prohibition in Mexico, and bar receipts at the track were never less than $5,000 a day. "What people really came to Tijuana for was the liquor," Coffroth admitted. "Whether the races were on or not, they poured over the border line—from 30,000 to 40,000 every Sunday and on holidays there were as many as 100,000 here. Labor Day was supposed to be the big day of the year. But actually

---

*With the usual confusion about Spanish names, Tijuana was variously spelled as Tiajuana or Tia Juana.

The Border's Open!

Every Day Oh, Muchacho!

Mon., Tues., Wed. American Legion Fiesta!

TIJUANA MEXICO

Diversions!

Fiesta Gaieties!

Barbecues!

Dining, Dancing, Cabaret SUNSET INN

-TIJUANA!

Let's Go!!

Plenty of Gasoline

Full Tanks Guaranteed

A newspaper enticement to visit south of the border, from 1920.

Sunday was. By Monday most of the crowd were too broke or too drunk to appear." The lines of cars drawn up at the border to return to the United States each Sunday were legendary. It was said you could walk from Tijuana to San Diego on their roofs.

When Prohibition was looming on the American horizon, Coffroth and his associates appreciated their position and began laying plans for expansion. Most important of the new investors Coffroth recruited was the colorful Baron Long who, like Coffroth, had been a fight promoter. Born in Indiana, Long had arrived in Los Angeles in 1908 and had partnered with former heavyweight champ Jim Jeffries in the Jeffries Athletic Club which staged club fights at the old Vernon Arena. In 1912, Long opened his famous Vernon Country Club, the first all-night nightclub in Southern California and a favorite with the film crowd. Entertainers like Abe Lyman and Gus Arnheim got their start at the Vernon C.C. and it was there, Long was fond of recalling years later, that he fired a male dancer who later achieved fame as Rudolph Valentino. Long opened Los Angeles' first Hawaiian theme restaurant, and, at various times, owned and managed the Sunset Inn at Santa Monica, the Nat Goodwin Cafe on the Goodwin Pier, and the famous Ship Cafe long a fixture of life in Venice. Long's most famous property was the one which gave him his greatest respectability: the Biltmore Hotel downtown.

Coffroth decided to develop a piece of land several miles from Tijuana, well-known by the local Indians for its excellent hot springs and mud baths. Here he built an immense spa and hotel with fifty bungalows, a dog racing track, a golf course, tennis courts, and a huge swimming pool lined with marble and reputed to have cost $750,000. Later, a horse racing track was added which seated 50,000 as opposed to the old track's 15,000.

Agua Caliente wasn't just a success, it was a smash hit and was expanded several times over the years until eventually it represented an investment of $10,000,000. The secret of Agua Ca-

liente's success was no secret at all. It was gambling. Coffroth and his wealthy associates had gone to Mexico City and had received the endorsement of two former presidents who, not surprisingly perhaps, became partners in the operation. A special bill was passed by the Mexican Senate allowing gambling in Baja California and giving the concession to Coffroth's group. With this, they created a "lavish citadel of joy."

The facilities were first class all the way. Long personally traveled to Europe to select the finest vintages for the wine cellar. Every room in the hotel had pink bathrooms and featured tortoiseshell toilet seats. The service in the hotel restaurant was gold. The track offered a total of $1,000,000 each year in purses which no track in North America could match. A 6,902-yard, par 72, championship golf course was created out of adobe. The highpoint of its year was the Agua Caliente Open with a first prize of $15,000, the largest single golf prize in the world.

Agua Caliente wasn't the only action in town. Night life flourished in Tijuana as well, although it was frequently of a different and markedly lower character. The Los Angeles Bar, Vernon Bar, Midnight Frolics, the San Francisco, Kentucky Barrel House and a score of others offered entertainments illegal most everywhere. The most notorious of them all was the Venus where, for two dollars and up, the girls would do most anything the customer desired with their clothes on or not.

The bar at the Commerciale was reputed to be 300 feet long — the largest in the world — and required fifteen bartenders at peak hours. The gambling games at the Foreign Club were supposedly on the level, though the rules and maximum bets were set much in the favor of the house. Black tie was de rigueur at Agua Caliente. At the Foreign Club anything would do.

It was at Agua Caliente that Baron Long perpetrated one of the great horse-betting coups of all time. The track permitted both parimutuel and book betting, and Long decided to take on the bookies. Long bet heavily on a favorite in one race, placing his bets at track odds with Eastern bookies. The odds on the horse began to fall toward less than even money. At the very last minute, Long had confederates bet a fortune on every other horse in the race, the result being that the odds on the favorite went up to 3–1. Long's horse won and the bookies were forced to pay. No one would have been the wiser had not Long taken great pleasure in recounting the story of his coup. The bad publicity forced him to resign his position as vice-president of the Jockey Club which ran the track.

The end for Agua Caliente came in 1935 when Mexican President Cardenas outlawed gambling. That, and the 1934 opening of horse racing at Santa Anita, finished the spectacular resort.

The island of Santa Catalina has had a checkered history. It was first discovered and named by the Spanish explorer Cabrillo who was responsible for much of the nomenclature around Southern California. Unfortunately, his discovery of the island was either overlooked or ignored by the next Spanish captain to arrive, Sebastian Viscaino, who proceeded to rediscover the island and, by right of rediscovery, rename it.

The island was a refuge for smugglers throughout the Spanish and Mexican periods, a good place to offload goods and ignore customs officials on shore. It was just as useful to modern smugglers during Prohibition. At night, residents of Avalon could hear the nearby whine of powerful speedboat engines as they ferried shipments of contraband from mother ships anchored out to sea to the mainland.

The island was given to an American, Thomas Robbins, as one of the very last acts of the last Mexican governor of California, Pio Pico. This was a generous act on Pico's part, though considering that he accepted a gift from Mr. Robbins for making it, one perhaps not beyond reproach. Between the 1850s and the 1890s, the island was held by various hands: no one could decide exactly what it might be good for. In late 1887, the then owner, James Lick, sold the island to one George Shatto. Shatto had the idea of developing it as a resort. He laid out a town and

his wife came up with a suitably romantic name for it: Avalon. Assumedly this Avalon is meant to recall Avallon which, in Arthurian legend, was an earthly paradise. Somewhere the spelling seems to have gone awry.

Shatto's plans did not fare well and, before too many years had passed, he was forced to sell the island. This time the purchasers were the Banning brothers. Their father, Phineas, was the man who had developed San Pedro as Los Angeles' port. The Bannings enjoyed their ownership of the island, building a fine residence there. To pay for this and all the improvements they made, they opened the island to the public as "a field for health and pleasure without counterpart in America or Europe."

By the 1890s, the tourist trade thrived. There was a formal hotel, the Metropole, and the Island Villa, a picturesque assortment of tent cabins priced at $1.50 a night for the basic arrangement, $2 for amenities like a wooden floor. The tent cities were a popular feature of Southern Californian summers for the next half century.

The Bannings profited from Catalina by charging tourists for transportation to the island. But gypsy boats tried to cut in on the trade and, by running a blockade set by the brothers, land passengers on the beach. These visitors would frequently be greeted by fire hoses and the Bannings weren't above wading into the surf and throwing interlopers in for a swim. The U.S. Post Office at Avalon was required by law to be accessible to all and not just those who'd paid the Bannings to get to the island. The arguments over the right to land at Catalina finally became so acrimonious that the Post Office was forced to relocate its office so that the backdoor was on the mean high tide line, land which was public. In this manner citizens could enter the building without setting foot on the Bannings' island.

Competition among the businesses on the island for the tourist trade was intense. Professional spielers were hired to hawk the services of glass-bottom boats and local cafes. Tourists might be literally shanghaied into seeing the island's famed underwater gardens. The Klondyke Cafe's

Avalon Bay, in the 1930s. The casino,
at right, was home to the nation's
finest big bands. And, at center, is the
S.S. *Catalina,* the Great White
Steamer, that daily brought hundreds
of tourists to the Magic Isle.

Catalina, California

Above. Downtown Avalon, Santa Catalina Island, in the 1930s. Avalon was exactly one mile square and contained the only land on the island not owned by Wrigley.

Below. Inside Island Villa, a temporary summer tent village, offering accommodations at $2 per night.

goes into ecstasy looking down," remarked an enthusiastic journalist.

In 1915, a disastrous fire came close to leveling the town of Avalon. The Bannings didn't have the funds to rebuild and so sold the island in 1919 to millionaire chewing gum magnate William Wrigley of Chicago. Mr. Wrigley loved the island. "Why it's wonderful!" he told the press. When Wrigley was asked how he planned to increase tourism to the island, something the Bannings had not been able to do, he remarked confidently: "If I can get people to chew my gum, I can get them to come to Catalina."

Wrigley cheerfully set about investing a fortune in the island. He brought out his Chicago Cubs baseball team and made the island their spring training grounds, a tradition which continued until the Avalon City Council fell afoul of Wrigley. They refused to put up the funds necessary to keep the training grounds green all year around, which Wrigley demanded for obscure reasons. For public relations value, Wrigley sponsored the first cross-channel swim, a grueling test that only one young man finished.

"I'm putting money into Catalina," Wrigley announced, "because I'm happy and I want others to be happy." Wrigley built the famous Casino, leveling the small Sugar Loaf Hill, a famous landmark, in the process. There never was any gambling at the Casino, only dancing. The finest of the big bands were booked there, from Benny Goodman to Jan Garber. Catalina became a regular stopover on the circuit of the major musical congregations. In the Casino's salad days, the ushers were formally dressed and, once, elegant Fred Astaire was refused admission because he wasn't wearing a tie.

These were the glory days of the stately Hotel St. Catherine, Hollywood's home away from home and one of its favorite trysting places, where the long noses of the hometown gossip columnists rarely protruded. Once, the night manager was summoned to the front desk. A certain Mr. Howard Hughes was angrily demanding a room despite having been told that the hotel was booked solid. He didn't need it for sleeping

hawker boasted his establishment was the only one with a real tree growing in the middle. This might be picturesque, conceded a rival spieler, but it wasn't very hygienic for a restaurant. The debates often ended in fisticuffs.

The delights of the Bar Harbor of Southern California were many. There was a golf course although it had oiled sand for greens. The glass-bottom boats were a perennial favorite: "One

Above. Venice: the Grand Lagoon which, at its prime, was clean enough to swim in.

Below. The Grand Lagoon, thirty years later, cemented in.

purposes; his yacht anchored in the harbor would do for that. It seemed ladies were balky about visiting gentlemen on their yachts late at night and a room ashore was needed for the convivial sports. Mr. Hughes was told again there were no rooms available.

People were forever leaving their loves in Avalon under the silvery moon. Al Jolson wrote the song which gave the island its greatest glory but it was really only one of many musical tributes.

Wrigley died in 1931 and his son, Philip, inherited the island. He was of a more baronial nature. When Mr. Wrigley, Jr. decided to take in a movie at the Casino, half of the house was roped off. After all, he owned every inch of the island except for the one square mile of the city of Avalon and, even there, he owned 80 percent of the land and had all his tenants on thirty-day discharge leases.

What gave Catalina its distinctive feel was the summer tourists. If you couldn't go anyplace else, you could still probably afford Catalina and, if not the hotels, the tent cities which sprang up. The guards employed there were students from UCLA and USC earning a few dollars and they were a particularly good source of information for the natives. Observing as they did all the "dollies," they could tell who had returned from the Casino with a partner and who alone.

Catalina was indeed the Magic Isle.

Venice-by-the-Sea, Venice of America as it was called, was the creation of a true eccentric, Abbot Kinney. Kinney's family made a fortune in the Gilded Age with a daring new product: cigarettes. Kinney's wealth freed him to search for a cure to the bane of his existence: insomnia. His search eventually led him to the healthful environment of Los Angeles, which he credited with curing him of the scourge.

Kinney became not only a resident but a booster. He authored a lengthy monograph on the eucalyptus tree which thrived in Southern California. With Helen Hunt Jackson, he wrote a study of the downtrodden Gabrielino Indians. And Kinney became a developer, purchasing a

Crowds were invited to ogle Madame Fatima who didn't just dance with her feet, or be amazed by the Snake Charmer or Bosco who "eats 'em alive!" Visitors could ride the miniature railway or the Whip, the Bamboo Dragon Slide, the Captive Aeroplanes, or go cascading Over the Falls. Most exciting were the roller coasters. First came the Race Through the Clouds, billed as one of the biggest in America, and later the Big Dipper, familiar to generations. There was a bathhouse with the world's largest salt water plunge and a ballroom of gargantuan proportions. With all this, Venice was transformed, the ads read, into "the beach closest to Los Angeles — the beach where you always find the brightest lights, the greatest thrills and the largest crowds of merrymakers."

The sights of Venice were well known, like the hotels along Windward Avenue which aped Italian architecture. If they weren't exactly authentic, they were as close as most people were going to get to the real thing. The Ship Cafe, built on pilings of its own alongside the pier, was a reproduction of the Spanish explorer Cabrillo's flagship. It was a colorful, popular, and hot, nightspot.

You could watch the movies being made outdoors around Venice, in fact sometimes it seemed as if most of Hollywood worked there. The airport was one of the first on the coast and the home of legendary stunt flyers. And there were the beauty contests which were held constantly: Miss Red Head, Auburn Hair Contest, Beautiful Back, Miss California or the contest to be Queen at Venice's annual revelry — the Mardi Gras — with a chance to rule alongside Old King Neptune and lead the parade along Ocean Front Walk.

Everybody played the Venice Ballroom so everybody danced there. Ben Pollock's congregations launched sidemen like Benny Goodman, Glen Miller, Gil Rodin and Jack Teagarden to fame and fortune. For those who preferred their dancing out-of-doors, there were the marathons which were illegal in Los Angeles but okay in Venice.

The heart of Venice was its pier, first built by

A dance marathon at the Venice Pier, ca 1924. However popular such contests might have been with the public, they were decidedly unwelcome in the eyes of the city council, which strenuously tried to block them. Jack "Doc" Kearns, legendary fight promoter and the brains behind Jack Dempsey and others, also staged the marathons. And when, in the late '20s, the council finally succeeded in its efforts to stop the marathons, it was only after the law arrested the dapper Kearns and tossed him in the cooler.

large tract of land immediately south of Santa Monica which he platted as the resort city of Ocean Park.

Along the line, Kinney had his great idea for yet another development. It would be called Venice of America and have picturesque cottages astride real canals, just like the other Venice. Located next door to Ocean Park, Kinney opened his dream city on July 4, 1905. "To See Venice Is To Live," Kinney advertised.

Somehow not all went well. The subdivision didn't prove profitable. Moreover, Kinney had in mind some social engineering. He hoped that supplementing the natural beauty of Venice with cultural events like Sarah Bernhardt and the Chicago Symphony would produce a Venice resident with an elevated outlook on life. In this he was disappointed.

Kinney retreated to trying to please the public's less elevated tastes. The Midway Plaisance was pure carny, a show imported from its successful run at the Portland's World Fair.

Above. Beauty contests were an almost weekly occurrence in Venice and Ocean Park. This one, in the mid-1920s, was to pick, well, a beauty.

Next page. Devastating pier fires and floods plus the discovery of oil combined to drastically alter the visionary Venice of America that had been the dream of Abbot Kinney.

Kinney, and extending 1,600 feet out to sea. A second pier, the Sunset Pier, was built north of the original one and linked to it to form a horseshoe. Still further north, on the boundary line between Ocean Park and Venice, was built Fraser's Million Dollar Pier, which opened in 1912. Later a second pier connected with it, Lick Pier.

Fire was a constant and spectacular problem for the piers. In 1920, a month after Kinney's death, his pier burned. His family pledged to rebuild it as rapidly as possible and reopened it six months later at a cost of $3,000,000. The Ocean Park or Fraser Pier burned twice in the 1920s.

Kinney made sure the spreading streetcar system connected to Venice. Beginning in 1904, you could get on what was eventually called the Venice Short Line downtown on Hill Street and, fifty minutes later, be at the ocean. The VSL was one of the most popular and hence profitable lines the Pacific Electric operated. In 1920, 5,500,000 passengers were carried. Sundays were inevitably big days and so was the Fourth of July and, when the Fourth fell on a Sunday, three-car trains had to be brought in to help ease the crushing load. Conductors also knew what to expect on the days when Venice held its annual Bathing Suit Parade,

on New Year's Eve, Halloween, and on Wednesdays, excursion days, when the fare was only 25¢.

The visitors had the time of their lives but Venice the city didn't fare so well. Warfare between straight-laced residents and the operators of the amusements was common. Early in the 1920s, the city treasurer absconded with the public purse. Police Chief Harry Raymond was accused of strongarm methods and eventually fired. Upstanding citizens blanched at the thought of what was rumored to go on at events like the Brownie's Ball. Public debate began over whether to end the city's independence and incorporate with either Santa Monica or Los Angeles.

In 1925, Venice became part of Los Angeles. Then the canals, which owing to poor design were not properly flushed by the ocean, became swamps. Los Angeles promised to rectify the situation but ended up doing so by filling in most of the canals.

The crushing blow to picturesque Venice was the discovery of oil. Wells sprang up, crowding out the residents, making the hardy few who remained inmates of an oil field. The merrymakers weren't affected. Throughout the Depression the fun rolled on. But by then, a tawdry Venice had come to replace the visionary Venice of America that had been the dream of Abbot Kinney.

Fatty Arbuckle's Plantation Cafe in
Culver City.

11

WHAT'S FOR BREAKFAST? LUNCH? DINNER?

"Easterner, if you folks from the East will eliminate heavy meats and potatoes and pastry from your diet, you will not have colds. You eat as if you were in the midst of a long, cold, winter. We natives who include more of our abundant fruits and vegetables in our diet are not troubled with colds." Signed, A Native

Although articles appeared regularly in Los Angeles newspapers boasting of the many "gastronomic adventures" available in the city of the angels, Los Angeles was not known for its cuisine. Those who presumed themselves to have taste in matters culinary turned their noses up at the city. Most notable was Willard Huntington Wright, former critic at large for the *Times*, who, in 1912, wrote a scathing indictment of city gastronomy entitled "Los Angeles — The Chemically Pure." Among the many and terrible deprecations Wright directed at the city, the worst was that the sum total of local gastronomic acuity consisted of an eternally cheery belief in "simplicity and quantity." "Cooking in Los Angeles," wrote Wright, "has none of the essentials of an art."

Which is not to say that Los Angeles did not have its contribution to make to the march of alimentary progress. But that contribution was not a distinctive cuisine nor a new style of cooking, neither a new method of preparation nor even a celebrated dish. Rather it was an institution, an eatery: the cafeteria.

The word "cafeteria" looks vaguely French but is vaguely Spanish. The word was around at least as early as the 1850s, when it represented a style of restaurant which came north from Mexico and which specialized in "ordinary alcoholic drinks and plain meals." In the 1920s, there were still cafeterias in the Mexican district of L.A. — Sonoratown — bunched along North Main Street. "The present cafeteria is of Mexican origin," wrote a visitor in the late 1920s. "The proprietors are mostly of a picturesque stoutness. They stand behind their counters and serve with such concentration and care that the gloomy, dingy atmosphere cannot dim their pride of ownership."

The cafeteria gave its name, if not much else, to another variety which was developed across town among the whites. Who first dreamed up the idea of displaying food for selection, having patrons push trays and help themselves, is uncertain. The first local cafeteria was that opened in 1905 by Miss Helen Mosher, on Hill Street between Third and Fourth. "All women cooks," she advertised, "food that can be seen," and, best of all, "no tips." The customer did all the work: selected his or her food, and returned the dirty dishes to the kitchen, although the public ultimately proved oblivious to this.

Mrs. Mosher was but a cafeteria visionary. It required other hands to develop the form to its fullest and elevate the cafeteria into the phenomenon it became. This genius was Horace Boos, born in Moscow, Ohio, aided by his three brothers, Cyrus, Henry and John. Horace Boos came to Los Angeles around 1905, just in time to observe Mrs. Mosher's efforts. He opened his first cafeteria a year later, on Second Street, between Broadway and Spring streets. As his biographer wrote thunderously in an epic pamphlet, *Glancing Back Along the Cafeteria Trail*, Boos "took the infant idea, enlarged upon it, saw as surely as may be seen in a vision it was practical, and proceeded to make it work." Mrs. Mosher was just a footnote, but the Booses, they were history.

Fellow restaurateurs laughed at the idea of the cafeteria. But the Boos brothers "saw the increasing tendency of women especially to 'shop' around," and planned on luring them with all manner of tempting foods plainly displayed. The Boos brothers invented fast food. Moreover, their idea defeated "the growing tipping evil. . . . The price of a tip would at least buy a piece of pie . . . and the four brothers proposed to sell pie and shortcake at a profit." The cafeteria was a clever response to inflation.

John Boos was the first Boos Brother Cafeteria chef. Cyrus was the butcher and Henry and Horace did the buying. The first of their cafeterias was one long rectangular room with the rear partitioned off as the kitchen. No breakfast was served, the dining room opened at 11:00 a.m. and closed at 2:00 p.m., reopening for dinner at 5:00. The first tray runners were wood, later replaced with tiled counters. At night an orchestra played. Bus boys were hired to take over returning the dishes.

Still the cafeteria had detractors. Grabeteria they called it. The Booses knew better: "The general public—from shop girls to attorneys, physicians, merchants and bankers—has placed its stamp of approval on the self-service place and it has come to stay."

By the mid 1920s, the Boos empire was at its greatest. There were six Boos Brothers Cafeterias across Los Angeles and one serving the summer crowd at Catalina. The flagship installation was on Hill Street, across from Pershing Square. It was designed "in the quaint style of English inns of 200 years ago" which must have made it look right at home in downtown Los Angeles. It had half-timbered work inside, wrought iron lanterns, subdued light although not candles, and a foyer outside the restrooms fit for barons and earls.

The Boos brothers served Los Angeles 3,000 bottles of milk a day, 800 pounds of fish every twenty-four hours, and 4,000,000 eggs per year. More than 1,000 steers each averaging 750 pounds went to their rewards knowing their remains were to be served to hungry Angelenos. Hogs, 1,422 of them weighing 200 pounds each, 1,178 more for hams alone, were brought to Boos kitchens and 40,800 broilers were sacrificed to satisfy the demand for fried chicken. At Christmas and Thanksgiving, 1,000 turkeys were dressed. By the mid 1920s, about 15 million people were being fed each year, this in a city of approximately 1,000,000.

The cafeteria was everything Los Angeles wanted to be but rarely was: clean and orderly and efficient and, if not exactly exciting, there was variety enough. It was reasonably priced and you weren't paying for silly frills. It was a good way to be out in public but be private at the same time. As Carey McWilliams noted, the cafeteria was a kind of "indoor picnic," and picnics were big in Los Angeles. So the cafeterias became "quasi-public institutions around which flourishing social life . . . revolved."

In 1929, the manager of one cafeteria hit on the plan of closing off a part of the dining room and reserving it for people attending one or an-

Left. Interior of a Boos Brothers Cafeteria, a Los Angeles holy place of sorts, in the mid-1920s.

Right. The interior of Clifford Clinton's Clifton's Cafeteria, South Seas edition. There is no indication that Clinton ever visited the South Seas and the source of his inspiration remains obscure.

other club meeting. The informal gatherings every cafeteria had witnessed now became slightly more formalized. Every Tuesday, the Nature Club of Southern California would meet and, on Fridays, it was the Sierra Club in what became poor man's banquets. The cafeteria became so closely associated with L.A. that one writer referred to Southern California as Sunny Cafeteria with absolutely no confusion in anybody's mind.

In 1926, Horace Boos died, a wealthy man. The spirit seemed to go out of the rest of the family. In early 1927, it was announced that the three surviving brothers had sold out their interest to the Childs Company, which operated a chain of 110 restaurants nationally. The Boos name, however, remained over the door until the last Boos Brothers Cafeteria folded.

Clifford Clinton was the next, and last, entry in the cafeteria Hall of Fame. Clinton, a descendant of New York governor DeWitt Clinton, was born in Berkeley, California, of parents both captains in the Salvation Army. For two years, he was a missionary in China, returning eventually to enter the restaurant business with his father. In 1931, he moved to Los Angeles and, with $2,000 in capital, opened his first cafeteria.

Clinton had a sure-fire idea for, as he called it, the Cafeteria of the Golden Rule. And that was: "Pay What You Wish — Dine Free Unless Delighted." In the depths of the Depression, the

people of Los Angeles were invited to dinner or lunch or breakfast at Clifton's, as his chain became known, and, if they didn't have the funds to pay the check, they paid what they had and, if they didn't like the meal, they could tear up the check. In one ninety-day period, Clinton served 10,000 free meals. One judge who dined at Clifton's told the owner: "This sounds fine to me. I am on the bench in Bankruptcy Court down the street. I give you just one year and then I expect to see you before me." Presumably the judge paid his full check.

Just as important as his pricing policy was Clinton's intuitive command of Los Angeles' deep-seated taste for the strange. In downtown L.A., Clinton renovated his cafeteria into Clifton's South Seas, a cafeteria out of *Rain* by way of Hollywood. The show began on the street where a towering facade featured real waterfalls and lush tropical plants in a display which loomed over the sidewalk. Inside were rooms decorated as thatched huts with neon palm trees, bamboo and wicker detailing, even one corner called the Rain Hut where, every twenty minutes, lights flashed and thunder sounded and water was heard pouring down as if the unwary customer, tray in hand, had been caught in a tropical rain storm. Around this South Seas splendor was wrapped Clinton's mildly evangelical Protestantism. There were lifelike statues of Christ and a

Meditation Room and, on every table, *Food for Thot*, a pamphlet of homespun wisdom and homily which appeared weekly in an edition of 32,000. Clifton's Brookdale, on South Broadway, was only slightly less spectacular. It featured trompe l'oeil depictions of a redwood forest, complete with a stream running through it. There was a waterfall, a wishing well, an old rock fireplace and an observation platform called the eagle's nest. Only in Los Angeles could you soar with the eagles and take along a lunch.

Cafeterias were not all Los Angeles had to offer gastronomically. Far from it. Outside their walls were other, and considerably more elaborate, institutions dedicated to dining. Los Angeles was becoming a place that liked to eat out. Even a city that liked to feast.

New Year's Eve was as gaily celebrated in Los Angeles as it was anywhere. The grand new Ambassador Hotel on Wilshire opened in time for New Year's Eve, 1921, but only just: ten minutes before midnight. The first real celebration was that for 1922. Three thousand revelers were in attendance: 1,400 at 259 tables in the main dining room, 1,012 at 180 tables in the fashionable Cocoanut Grove and another 500 in the Zinnia Grill. Thirty-five captains oversaw the efforts of 250 waiters and 75 bus boys. In the Grove and Grill, huge decorative clocks stood and, at midnight, to the sound of trumpets, the clock faces swung open and ballet dancers glided out to lead merrymakers in a dance to the New Year. A parade of chefs snaked through the mobs, each carrying an electrically illuminated tray with a letter carved from ice: HAPPY NEW YEAR the line spelled out.

At the Alexandria downtown, which, until the opening of the Ambassador, had been *the* fashionable L.A. hotel, 800 guests jammed the main dining room. At midnight, a girl dressed as a chicken "flew" onto a table in front of a large mock clock and, singing "Cock-a-doodle doo," greeted the New Year: "The old year is dead, welcome to the new. Get up, we'll dine and sup, a toast to 1922." Whereupon the clock opened to reveal a scantily clad young lady reclining on a

Above. The front of the souvenir wine list from the fashionable Ambassador Hotel.

Below. The cover of the menu from Frank Sebastian's New Cotton Club, "In the Heart of Screenland" in Culver City.

MAIN DINING ROOM
The AMBASSADOR
Los Angeles
BEAM 501

The dining room at the Ambassador in the days of its earliest glamour, ca 1925.

Next page. A menu from the heyday of Roscoe "Fatty" Arbuckle's Plantation Cafe in Culver City, where the elite of Hollywood's movie colony were rewarded, after the long drive to the distant roadhouse, by Queen Olives, Chateau Briand for $4, and Zucchini Florentine.

half moon.

The Valley Hunt Club was packed as were the Annandale, Midwick and Altadena Country Clubs. In Pasadena, the stately Green and equally elegant Raymond Hotels were the center of attention. One perennial question was where the teams in town for the New Year's Day Rose Bowl would be feted. In 1922, the University of California was hosted at the Maryland Hotel while rival team, Washington and Jefferson, was at the Vista Del Arroyo. Both banquets must have been equally good for, the next day, the teams tied 0-0.

A good time at a high class hotel anytime in the '20s cost upward of $10. A more reasonable if less spectacular repast, including a dance, was available at a quality restaurant like Marchetti's at Western and Fifth for $7.50. The Chinese Gardens in Hollywood were still more reasonable at $5 a plate. The Tavern, atop picturesque Mt. Lowe, offered New Year's turkey dinner for a mere $1.50. But you had to include the $2 round-trip Red Car fare it was going to cost to get there and probably a room for the night.

Venice was a good place to spend New Year's Eve. There was dancing in the streets and no cover at the colorful Ship Cafe. Nearby in wide-open Culver City, Frank Sebastian's Cotton Club offered dinner de luxe and a show for $2.50, but there was also a $3 cover charge. Even so, for $5.50, you got "Plantation melodies, jazz, dancing, syncopation, dining, entertainment furnished by real Southern colored entertainers."

A more modest repast was available at Carl Jahnke's coffee shop on West 9th: $1 for a turkey dinner, although that rose to $1.25 by 1925, but was back to $1 by 1928. The turkey dinner at the New Hotel Rosslyn at Fifth and Main featured "Imperial Valley milk-fed young turkeys" with all the trimmings for $1.50, although the regular 50¢ dinner was also available. The semi-elegant Arcady Apartment Hotel in the mid-Wilshire area offered a dinner and musical in its Pompeiian Room. There was a choice of lamb, New York sirloin, half spring chicken or turkey, relish tray, asparagus tips hollandaise or new peas au beurre, duchesse or sweet potatoes, a salad, and hot mince pie, Apple Charlotte pudding, or ice cream and a demitasse all for $2. Add cream of fresh tomato or consommé en tasse, filet mignon instead of New York sirloin, zucchini florentine and English plum pudding, and you had the considerably more elegant fare at the Victor Hugo, in the 1920s, probably Los Angeles' most notable restaurant. The table charge rose to $3.

Probably the best bargain was at John Tait's Coffee Shop on South Broadway which advertised soup, including chicken gumbo with okra; cocktail choice, including California oyster; creamed chicken à la king or two grilled lamb chops or mixed grill or turkey with chestnut stuffing, pan gravy and cranberry sauce or young Jersey pig; and pie or cake or pudding with cheese plus milk, tea, coffee or beer all for only $1.

As the decade of the '20s progressed, one issue that was increasingly debated when it came time to toss out the old and hail the new, was how much booze would be available to grease the festivities. In 1924, Prohibition officers insisted "the only liquor available in Los Angeles is synthetic Scotch and gin and homemade wine." The Associated Press, on the other hand, announced that 1,800 cases of Canadian whiskey had been

landed in Santa Barbara and trucked in to Los Angeles. It was all a matter of who you thought knew booze best: the authorities or the press. L.A. Police Chief Lee Heath hit upon a flawlessly Hollywood way of scaring Prohibition into Los Angeles. He told the press and the press told the people, that scattered in and among the gayest New Year's celebrations would be an underground army of police officers in strictly plain clothes: "a bevy of feminine police operatives in fetching evening gowns... escorted by full-dressed detectives... sleuths disguised as waiters and taxi chauffeurs." This may have scared some but everybody realized that, while any denizen of the detective bureau could probably have delivered a flawless performance of a waiter or a cab hack, where was the dick who could pull off full, fancy dress? Or, if they could pull off full dress, it was very unlikely they could get away with wearing it.

With the Depression, the conversation changed to how much revelry one could get for how little. Holiday turkey dinner at the Rosslyn fell to 75¢, still with all the trimmings. At Frank Sebastian's, $3.50 now got you dinner, but there was no cover, and there were four different shows featuring a cast of "42 Glorified Creole Artists," the Les Hite Cotton Club Band, Henry Star, the "Hot Spot of Radio," and three different dance floors.

The Club Montmartre offered for Christmas, 1933, a de luxe dinner plus a free bottle of wine for $1.50. If that was too much, there was turkey dinner at Boos Brothers Cafeteria, for 40¢. Or at either of two Clifton's locations, where "It's Not An Extravagance," turkey dinner cost 52¢.

The popular Lucca Italian restaurant, which had a branch in San Francisco, offered a concert orchestra and the chance to be on radio since both KNX and KMTR broadcast from there: New Year's Eve dinner only $1.50 and "you can always ask for more." In 1935, at the depths of the Depression, New Year's Eve at the popular Palomar Ballroom, the former El Patio on Third and Vermont, was $5 a person. But for $5 you got: a private table, de luxe dinner, champagne cocktail, party favors, three floor shows and two bands including Mariscal's Merrymen and the popular cutup, Joe Venuti and his Venutians. Traditional duck dinner downtown at Taix was 75¢ or, if you wanted one of their famous private booths, $1. By 1936, things were really grim at Sebastian's. You could get Duke Ellington and his band and a turkey dinner for $1 and still no cover.

Not everyday was a holiday. Dinner at Brittingham's Radio Center restaurant in the brand new CBS-KNX building on El Centro and Sunset cost 75¢ for the Steak Hamburger KNX. The KNX cocktail, ingredients unspecified, was an additional 40¢. Down the street, Mike Lyman's featured a huge menu: twenty-one fish items including abalone steak at 85¢ and lobster for $1, and twenty-one meat items including double porterhouse steak for $2.50 and combination grill for 90¢. Green turtle soup was 40¢, Coos Bay clams on the half shell 60¢, and all mixed drinks, 25¢. Competing Al Levy's, one of the oldest restaurants in L.A. offered a twenty-ounce New York steak for $2.

Levy's did well through the 1930s but the heart had gone out of the restaurant business as far as Al Levy was concerned. Prohibition, and then the Depression, had killed dining: "People have forgotten how to dine," Levy said, "they merely eat." Levy liked to remember the good old days when his fabled establishment at Third and Main was the most famous cafe on the Coast and could serve a banquet to 1,500 people. Then, the menus were long and banquets were an all-night affair. And people dressed. "People once dressed to go to the theater but do not to go to the movies, and the diamonds they loved to display in gilded cafes are now in hock or safety deposit boxes."

Part of the problem was that nobody was quite sure what to wear because, whereas in Levy's day restaurants Frenchified cuisine, Los Angeles was now an international city. There were good Greek cafes on Fourth Street between Main and Los Angeles streets. On Spring, north of Fifth, were Hungarian kosher restaurants, and a mass of kosher Jewish restaurants in East Los Angeles. There had been German restaurants since the days the Turnverein was popular. Chinese restaurants were in Chinatown, naturally, and Japanese clustered around First Street in Little Tokyo. Russian inns were to be found in East L.A. and in Hollywood, most operated by white Russians. It was different from Al Levy's day. But just as good.

The Los Angeles Angels open their
1937 season.

12

THE SPORTS CAPITAL OF THE KNOWN UNIVERSE

It didn't take a public relations genius to figure out that part of the appeal of Los Angeles was that it was a paradise for the sports fan. All conceivable sports were played here and all the Chamber of Commerce needed to add was that they were being played year around. It happened that, at the moment the Chamber was saying this, America was in the throes of sports mania.

Golf. Americans went golf crazy in the 1920s. The game had gotten its start in Los Angeles in 1897. The first course was built near Pico and Alvarado and featured greens constructed from sand, tomato cans sunk in the ground as cups and lots of gophers. From these humble beginnings arose the socially prestigious Los Angeles Country Club.

By the mid-1920s, there were twenty-four private courses in Southern California and two excellent municipal ones at Griffith Park which had to be closed due to anthrax. The first Los Angeles Open was played in 1926, and there was a major tournament across the border at Tijuana. The L.A. Junior Chamber of Commerce wasn't being just poetic when it enthused: "Long holes over generous fairways, requiring a smacking drive and raking brassie to the green. Fascinating one shot holes form a wooded knoll to the doily of a green. This has been golf ne plus ultra."

Polo. One day, *Our Gang* producer Hal Roach saw polo being played at Midwick Country Club. Smitten by the game, he learned it and spread the infection to the rest of his industry cronies. Polo became the unofficial sport of Hollywood.

One Roach convert was Will Rogers who became obsessed. He sank $100,000 into a playing field and $50,000 into a stable of ponies. It cost at least $5,000 a year to play the game which was no burden to, among others: Jack Warner, Walt Disney, Darryl Zanuck, Johnny Mack Brown, Spencer Tracy and Robert Montgomery. The snobbishness traditionally associated with polo made it perfect for nouveau riche Hollywood.

Pro Football. The idea which made professional football a paying sports attraction belonged to C. C. Pyle, Cash and Carry Pyle, the greatest sports promoter of his generation.

On the left, Red Grange, the Galloping Ghost with his mentor, friend, agent and banker, C.C. "Cash and Carry" Pyle.

Pyle was an obscure theater owner in Champagne, Illinois, and there he might have remained were it not for the fact that Harold "Red" Grange played football for the nearby University of Illinois. In the early 1920s, the American public fell in love with college football chiefly by following the exploits of Grange, the Galloping Ghost. When Grange's undergraduate days were done, there was no place for him to go. But C.C. made Red a proposition. C.C. would make him a millionaire. All Red had to do was play football.

Pyle took his client to George Halas, the player-coach of the struggling pro team, the Chicago Bears. Red could inject into the near moribund pro game all the thrills of college ball. Pyle didn't merely drive a hard bargain, he held Halas up, and Poppa Bear was smart enough to recognize the wisdom of what C.C. was saying.

Grange, who had hardly seen $50 in one place, was handed a check for $25,000. He folded it up and carried it around for days to make sure nobody was going to ask for it back. Grange played his first pro game on Thanksgiving, 1925, for which he and C.C. were paid $7,000. The first season was a big success, Pyle and Grange splitting 25 percent of every dollar Halas made after deducting stadium rentals.

Red Grange cut up the playing fields and now C.C. did the same down the playing field of American advertising. There was $5,000 for Red endorsing a dairy, $3,500 for Red in a certain kind of sweater, and $1,000 for his endorsing a brand of cigarettes. Grange did not, of course, smoke. "I could only say," he admitted, "that, for all I knew to the contrary, if I were a smoker, there was no reason why I shouldn't smoke these pills."

Red, C.C. and a team of Chicago Bears brought their pro football roadshow to Los Angeles in January, 1927. The red carpet was rolled out for the Wheaton Whirlwind. A crowd jammed the train station to greet him and 100 of the city's elite took him to lunch at the Biltmore. It wasn't that he was a genuine hero, it was the constantly reiterated stories of just how much money he was making for his heroics.

A crowd of 70,000 paid their way into the Coliseum to see Grange take on a pick-up team, dubbed the Los Angeles Tigers and led by George Wilson, a former All-American at the University of Washington. Damon Runyon was on hand marveling at the sports-minded Los Angeles public. Grange and the Bears easily beat the Tigers 17-7. A breathless recantation followed, not of the scoreboard but of the cashbox. Grange got $50,000 for this one afternoon. Pro football was a helluva game.

The Bunion Derby. C.C loved Los Angeles. When it came to his biggest, most spectacular promotion, C.C. could think of no better place than this fair city. The Bunion Derby was a marathon, the world's greatest, the winner the first one to New York City.

Charley Pyle was sure he could make it pay. Why, you couldn't tell the runners apart without a program and he'd print the programs. Then, he'd be out in front of the pack, selling to small towns the right to have the race come right down their main streets. "Each town will be assessed by me for advertising or we won't run through it," C.C. announced. "We'll run through a rival town. You know what that means."

On March 4, 1928, the greatest grind of them all set out from Ascot Speedway in East Los Angeles. Two hundred seventy-six runners prepared to take to New York and America the message that this was the Golden Age of the Foot, for Charley Pyle said so. The message bearers weren't the world-class runners C.C. had envisioned. One newspaper noted: "No sporting event ever drew a stranger entry list." There was one cowboy complete with boots, a sixteen year old, a sixty-five year old, Harry Abramowitz of New York, next to one Constantinoff who listed home as Siberia.

The first few days were the hardest owing to the blazing heat of the desert east of the city. Olli Kolehmainen, the holder of every world mark from five to ten miles and the biggest name C.C. could persuade to enter, dropped out. After ten days, the field was down to 127 unknowns, one runner having been struck by a car.

Yessir, Horace Greeley Started Something
By Webb Smith

Above left, the start of the First Bunion Derby, and *right,* two weary entrants. *Below.* The ignominious failure of the First Bunion Derby made Corn and Callous Pyle's audacious announcement of a second Derby a year later a newsworthy item.

for free. Each night, C.C. would set up a carnival but the entertainment, which included one runner's imitation of a steamboat whistle, wasn't drawing the crowds. Worst was that one runner, a young Oklahoma boy, Andrew Payne, established so great a lead he couldn't be beat. When the race ended, 3,400 miles from L.A. in new York, it was dubbed "The most heroic, if one of the most absurd, athletic contests ever held."

For some curious reason, the following year, C.C. decided to do it all again, only from New York to Los Angeles. This time, lightning struck and the Bunion Derby turned into a horserace. John Salo, a former cop from Passaic, New Jersey, who'd placed second in the first Derby, was head-to-head with Peter Gavuzzi, an English long-distance runner. On Sunday, June 16, 1929, the runners tore into Wrigley Field for the last leg of the Derby, a standard twenty-six-mile-plus marathon. After nine miles, Salo passed Gavuzzi and went on to win—by 2 minutes and 47 seconds after 3,000 miles. Ironically, spectators insisted Gavuzzi had lost at least that much time in Long Beach, trying to cross the street on the way to Wrigley Field and avoid being hit by a PE Red Car.

Baseball. The Pacific Coast League, the PCL, was minor league in name only. In the quality of its players, it equaled the big leagues. The PCL season began about March and ran until November, which meant 200 and more games per season, 50 more than the majors.

The league was founded in 1903 and the first champs were from Los Angeles. The team was called the Loos-Loos and then the Angels which was objected to by a local minister. His objection was overruled.

L.A.'s great rival team was the Vernon Tigers, owned by the beer-brewing Maier family. The Tigers played Sundays and Tuesdays in Vernon, at a field so close to Jack Doyle's famous saloon that the centerfielder could, and did, duck out for a short beer between innings. The high point of the Tiger-Angel rivalry came in 1919, when the teams were one, two in the standings coming into a seven-game, head-to-head series

There were complaints. The runners said C.C. wasn't providing the first-class accommodations he'd promised. "His dietician was an old-time can opener from the army," said one runner, "who would toss a lot of old meat into a pot and say, 'Nice juicy steaks for supper tonight, boys.'"

Charley had other problems. Nobody was paying him since everybody could see the race

Left. The greatest Angel of them all, Arnold "Jigger" Statz, who, in addition to his achievements on the diamond, was also the golf champ of the Pacific Coast League.

Center. Fan's eye view of the action at the old Wrigley Field, home of the L.A. Angels. Unlike its namesake in Chicago, this field had lights and night baseball.

Right. Outside Gilmore Field. Only in 1939, with the opening of Gilmore did the Hollywood Stars actually play their games in Hollywood.

that would decide it all. The Angels needed to win two of seven. A crowd of 22,000 jammed their home field, Chutes Park on Washington and Main, and watched L.A. as it failed to win more than one game. In 1926, the Tigers sold to San Francisco interests and moved to that city where they became the Missions.

Next, club owner Bill Lane brought his Salt Lake City team to L.A. where it was renamed the Stars and played for Hollywood. Hollywood had a series of lackluster seasons until 1929. The team to beat that year was the Missions who had hitters like Ike Boone, on his way to a batting crown with a .407 average. The Missions could never quite nail the season down and eventually were forced into a climactic series with the Stars. Hollywood walked away with its first ever championship.

The Angels were a powerhouse team in the 1920s and 1930s. The Serifs, as they were called, won five league championships, including the amazing 1934 season when the team won 137 games for a .732 average. Their championship was so unchallenged that, instead of a final series, the league pitted them against a team of PCL All-Stars. The Angels won that series 4-2.

Part of the reason for the Angels' successes was Arnold "Jigger" Statz, an Angel for eighteen seasons. He set the all-time PCL mark for most games played (2,790), most at bats, most hits, doubles, triples and runs scored. He is the only

man in the history of baseball, major or minor, to have handled 500 put outs in each of three seasons. And he's generally given credit for having played in more professional baseball games than any other man.

In 1935, the Hollywood Stars moved to San Diego and, two years later, the Missions returned and became a new Hollywood Stars team. Despite the fact the Stars played for Hollywood, their home field was the Angel ballpark, Wrigley Field on Santa Barbara and 54th Street. In 1939, Gilmore Field was built next to Gilmore Stadium and the Farmer's Market and, for the first time, the Stars actually played in Hollywood.

Boxing. In the 1890s, the heavyweight champion of the world was a San Franciscan: Gentleman Jim Corbitt. And the big man in the ring in the early part of the century was James J. Jeffries of Los Angeles. By the '20s and '30s, Los Angeles was a center of the sweet science.

The great promoters were men like Uncle Tom McCarey whose son, Leo, became one of the great Hollywood directors. McCarey promoted fights at Naud Junction, the intersection of Main, Alhambra and Macy streets downtown, named for a baker who had his oven nearby.

After Jack Doyle erected a new arena in Vernon, McCarey moved there, and Vernon became the heart of Western boxing. In 1914, however, California outlawed prize fighting. Joe Rivers and Johnny Dundee fought the last twenty-round

Fidel La Barba in his prime, the
Flyweight Champion of the World.

bout at Vernon in December of that year.

Doyle kept the fight game alive during the ensuing dark age by organizing four-round exhibition bouts. The only prizes supposedly being given out were medals, which were worn smooth from being handed back and forth.

The Vernon arena seated 4,000 and was a dimly lit wooden structure with chicken wire between the ring and bleachers to keep zealous fans from staging impromptu bouts. The air would be thick with blue cigar smoke as fighters like Midget Smith or Bert Colima slugged it out. The benches always included the greats of the movie industry: the Keystone Kops and their producer, Mack Sennett, Mabel Normand, Charlie Chaplin, Ben Turpin, Chester Conklin and Fatty Arbuckle who had a special reserved seat 50 percent wider to fit his massive girth.

The crowds got so big that Doyle had to pull down the old Vernon arena and build a new one. It seated 10,000 and opened August 28, 1923, before a glittering crowd. The ring was jammed with floral decorations and the audience spontaneously broke into singing, "Hail, Hail, the Gang's All Here." "It was a crowd that couldn't be duplicated outside of Los Angeles or New York," observed one writer. "Thousand-dollar-a-week movie actors rubbed elbows with timid pork and bean extras, millionaires and newsboys stepped on each other's feet good-naturedly, and beautiful society women gazed haughtily across the aisles at 1924 model vampires just out of the paint shop."

As brightly as Vernon shone, brighter still was the Olympic Auditorium which opened downtown in 1925. That house seated 15,000 in more comfort than fight fans had traditionally been accorded. There were no pillars blocking anybody's view, ample lights, and huge fans which made lingering cigar smoke a thing of the past. Before long, Doyle was moving the heart of L.A. boxing to the Olympic. Vernon was abandoned and, in 1927, in what was described as one of the more spectacular fires in recent memory, it burned to the ground.

Another great local boxing monument was George Blake, trainer of champions and referee. In the 1920s, Blake taught boxing at the L.A. Athletic Club and it was there he met and trained his greatest champ, Fidel "Fiddle" La Barba.

La Barba's family had come from Abruzzi, Italy, and he was born in New York. The family moved to L.A. in 1914 and, not long afterward, Fidel's mother died. His father was left to raise thirteen children.

As a newsboy, Fidel sold the *Express* which he remembered as "a tough paper to sell so they had to pay you to hustle them." Fidel's hustle put him on a corner where a taller boy was selling another newspaper. When a passerby went for the other vendor Fidel would run up and push his way in. The opposition would eventually take a swing and Fidel, despite his size, would flatten him.

In 1924, George Blake took his pupil to the national amateur tournament and Fidel won, which automatically placed him on the Olympic team. Fidel took the gold in the flyweight division in the 1924 London Olympics. In the wake of his victory, La Barba debated whether to accept a scholarship he'd been offered at Stanford or turn professional. He decided to box, and George Blake became his manager.

The following year, world flyweight champ Frankie Genaro came out from New York looking for an easy title defense. He gave La Barba the shot. La Barba was certainly a sentimental pick to beat Genaro. The odds, however, were with Genaro who, like Fidel, had been the Olympic flyweight champ. The match was staged outdoors at Ascot, August 22, 1925.

Genaro was cocky. "I look for a tough fight," he said, "but I can't lose." He was half right. La Barba methodically worked Genaro over and, when the final bell sounded, he was the victor.

The crowd surged deliriously into the ring. La Barba threw his arms around Blake and kissed him. "George Blake did it for me," he told the press. "But for him I'd be one of the ordinaries." The happy mass of humanity made it impossible for Fidel to get to his dressing room. Six burly policemen charged forward, one lifting Fidel up

on his shoulders to carry him out. Eighteen years old, president of his class at Lincoln High, and now flyweight champion of the world.

Fidel's father, who didn't approve of his son's interest in fighting, nervously refused to attend the match or listen to it on the radio. He found out the outcome the way most of L.A. did: when frenzied newsboys took to the streets with special editions announcing one of their own had fought his way to the top.

For a few years, Fidel successfully defended his title and then retired, undefeated, to enter Stanford. But he stayed at school for only one year. Friends convinced him, he said, he was turning his back on a mountain of cash.

The next several years were grueling ones for La Barba. The nemesis of his attempted comeback was the Cuban, Eligio Sardinias, known as Kid Chocolate. In 1929, the Kid narrowly defeated Fidel. A year and a half later, Fidel was the victor and eventually got a shot at the title holder, Bat Battalino. La Barba went into the fight a 2½ – 1 favorite but Battalino had a knack of beating the odds. In a relentless attack that surprised the experts, Battalino won a unanimous decision.

In December, 1932, La Barba again met Kid Chocolate who now held the featherweight title. It was a hard, fifteen-round match. What no one outside of Fidel's camp realized was that La Barba had, in training, torn the retina in his left eye. The scrappy La Barba went down to defeat, a defeat which effectively ended his career. Later, after unsuccessful surgery, he lost his eye.

At the other end of the boxing world was Ace Hudkins. Nicknamed the Nebraska Wildcat, he made Los Angeles his home. Pasty-faced and blue-eyed, Hudkins was a brawler: few moves, no science, some ability to deliver a punch but, most important, an endless ability to take punishment. Ace Hudkins was a human punching bag and he won his fights by being the last guy in the ring standing up.

Hudkins began fighting in 1923 and, in 1928, got his first big break: a middleweight shot against the stylish Mickey Walker. Walker, who spent a lot of time in L.A., was a fashion plate, friend of Al Capone, and a smart boxer who eventually held the welterweight and middleweight titles. His manager was the colorful Jack Kearns, who had managed Dempsey and, from time to time, promoted marathon dances in L.A. and Venice. Dempsey once told Walker: "Mickey, you'll make millions with Kearns but you'll die broke. Money to him is just something to spend for a good time."

The first Hudkins-Walker brawl was fought in Chicago, in a downpour. Walker was lucky to win. The second contest came a year and a half later at Wrigley Field in Los Angeles. More than 21,000 paid to see Walker disassemble Hudkins. Ace retired a few years later and, with his brothers, formed a company which supplied horses to the movies.

Left. The Human Buzz-saw and one of the greatest of all time, Henry Armstrong, 1936.

Right. Henry Armstrong in the ring at the height of his career. In a notable episode, his contract was purchased by singer Al Jolson, a long-time boxing enthusiast.

But the greatest of them all, one of the all-time greats, was the man they called Homicide Hank, Henry Armstrong. Born into a sharecropper's family in St. Louis, Armstrong grew up tough, and fought amateur and then professional fights. With the Depression, he decided to move to Los Angeles.

He spent months living in charity houses, eating off bread lines, and haunting the gyms — the Manhattan, the Ringside, the Main — hoping for a chance. Finally, he got a spot again as an amateur. Turning professional for a second time, Armstrong fought and was twice defeated by the Mexican, Baby Arizmendi. Nothing came easy to Henry Armstrong. Then, in 1927, he defeated Petey Sarron and became featherweight champ. Now he hit his stride.

Armstrong was inexhaustible. He threw punch after punch, never stopping until the bell sounded. They called him the Human Buzz-saw. And when he threw punches, he threw them with all the muscle he'd developed slinging a sledgehammer on the railroad.

The year following his victory over Sarron, Armstrong went up in weight to meet Barney Ross for the world's welterweight championship and Henry won. Then, incredibly, he took the lightweight title from Lou Ambers to become the only man in ring history to that point to hold three titles simultaneously.

It was impossible to keep up with the demands of the various weight classifications. Late in '39, he gave up the featherweight title, and then was defeated in a rematch against Ambers for the lightweight crown.

In March, 1949, Armstrong went into the ring for the greatest battle of his career, against Ceferino Garcia for the world middleweight championship. No man before or since held four different titles.

Despite the fact that Garcia outweighed Armstrong, Homicide Hank tore into the champ. It was Armstrong all the way, at least that's what they said at ringside. But when the fight was over, George Blake, the referee and sole judge, raised Garcia's hand. Blake said Armstrong had only a slight lead in rounds, and that he had repeatedly fouled the champ. Armstrong insisted he'd been robbed, that somebody had fixed the fight. George Blake never refereed again. Henry Armstrong retired without his illusive fourth title.

College Football. When, after World War I, America went college football crazy, being a great school meant having a great team. USC didn't have a great team and that was intolerable to Los Angeles boosters.

Elmer "Gloomy Gus" Henderson had an excellent record coaching high school ball when, in 1919, USC hired him. His first season was closely watched, especially when he took his new team up against California and its legendary coach, Andy Smith. The good news was the battle drew the then huge crowd of 9,000. The bad news was Cal won. The following year, Henderson and his team went undefeated but they didn't have to play Cal. Cal, meanwhile, was national champion.

In 1921, 25,000 were on hand when Cal met USC. It was one of those games sports writers like to say was closer than the score, 38-7 in favor of Cal in this case. At least USC was admitted to the Pacific Coast Conference, recognition that, in sports, it had arrived.

In 1922, USC was defeated only by Cal. And when Andy Smith magnanimously declined a third straight invitation to play the Rose Bowl, USC got the nod. The game against Penn State was controversial, the coaches almost coming to blows over Penn State's alleged stalling tactics.

Above. The UCLA football team huddles around coach Bill Spaulding, 1935.

Below. Howard Jones, USC football genius, explains the finer points of the game to his 1937 squad.

The Nittany Lions dallied at the parade, hoping to put off the start of the game until the blistering sun had partially set.

In '23 and '24, USC again failed to beat Cal. Moreover, both Cal and Stanford were angered at the upstart Southern California institution, feeling that what USC lacked in academic excellence it was trying to make up for with a flashy football team. Matters reached a head when, immediately prior to the Cal-USC game at Berkeley, USC officials were handed a note informing them that, after the current season, both Cal and Stanford intended on severing athletic relations with the Trojans. Humiliated, USC went on to lose to Cal 7-0.

USC boosters were infuriated and resolved to suffer no further indignities on the playing field. Gus Henderson's record wasn't bad, but he was let go in favor of Howard Jones. Jones was one of the masters of college coaching, coming off two undefeated seasons at Iowa, including a spectacular upset which ended a Notre Dame streak.

With its new coach, USC acquired a new persona. The team now organized around All-American, triple-threat man, Morley Drury, was dubbed The Thundering Herd. Jones' first year as coach was a great success dimmed only by a 13-6 loss to Stanford before 70,000 at the Coliseum.

Not long after Jones arrived, USC had a great idea: to arrange a yearly game with Notre Dame. When the already legendary Knute Rockne was approached about the idea, he was lukewarm. But upon consideration of how pleasant a trip to the sunny West Coast in the middle of the Midwestern winter could be, he agreed. It would be the first major intersectional match up ever outside a bowl. The first game was played December 4, 1926, in a sold-out Coliseum.

Derailed on his way to a national championship by an upset, Rockne wasn't about to lose this first game. On the eve of the game, he sadly told the press his poor boys were exhausted in an attempt to inject the Trojans with overconfidence.

It was a furiously contested game. In the second quarter, Notre Dame scored. The try for

UNIVERSITY OF SOUTHERN CALIFORNIA   LOS ANGELES, CAL. 786

The home turf of L.A.'s two rivals: USC in the late 1920s, and UCLA in 1937, after the move from the old Southern Campus on Vermont, to a new facility in Westwood Village.

the extra point was partially blocked. Ironically, the block may have helped the ball pass the goal. Later, USC had a point after blocked. And, in the fourth quarter, Morley Drury, the man they called The Noblest Trojan of Them All, attempted a point after which hit the uprights and bounced back onto the field. That was the margin of difference as USC lost 13-12.

The game had electrified the nation and it was no surprise that the second edition, played at Soldier's Field, Chicago, was attended by 120,000, the largest crowd ever to see a college game.

In the first quarter, each team scored but, once again, USC failed in an attempt at a point after. The game settled into a 7-6 defensive battle until late in the fourth quarter when USC threatened. Morley Drury uncorked a pass intercepted by Notre Dame's Charles Riley. As he started to run forward, he was hit and fumbled the ball into the end zone where it was recovered by USC. Two points for Troy! Only the referee, John Schommer, saw it differently and ruled the play an incomplete forward pass. USC lost 7-6. After viewing films of the game, Schommer was repentent: "It looks like I pulled a boner," he told the press.

In 1928, USC went undefeated, was tied only by Cal, and finally beat Notre Dame 27-14. The next year, the Trojans were smarting from yet another upset at the hands of Cal which cost them their second straight number one rating. They had been replaced by—guess who?—Notre Dame and a victory over the Irish would put them back on top. Before another sellout in Chicago, once again a missed extra point cost them the game, 13-12.

In 1930, despite being a favorite, USC again lost. So when 1931's renewal came around, USC was hungry. The game was played against a remarkable emotional background for, in the spring of that year, Knute Rockne had died. And now, his team was one victory away from yet another national championship.

In the third quarter, it had been Notre Dame all the way. Suddenly, the Trojans caught

fire. USC ran for a touchdown but failed to make the point after. When the Trojans got the ball back, they scored again.

With three minutes to play and the score Notre Dame 14 and USC 13, quarterback Gus Shaver unleashed a desperation fifty-yard pass which, amazingly, was caught. But, at the Notre Dame 17, USC's drive was halted. It looked hopeless. Kicker Johnny Baker was called into the game. He had never kicked a field goal all season. As the two-minute warning was given, Baker knew that, if he missed, he could never return to Los Angeles. He didn't miss.

The train carrying the Trojans home was hailed by fans who had heard the game on the radio. When it pulled into L.A., the team got a real surprise. A crowd estimated at 300,000, a third of the entire city, was on hand to celebrate the victory with a parade through downtown. It was the greatest sports-minded congregation in the city's history.

Joe College was as comfortably at home on the USC campus as he would have been at a more traditional emblem of undergraduate bliss like Notre Dame. USC was cast in the Midwestern mold. Social life on campus revolved around the fraternities and sororities—there were thirteen for the ladies alone. Members were barred from drinking, smoking and wearing bobbed hair. Freshmen all had to have a copy of the Freshman Bible with them at all times while on campus and it included strict caveats such as no smoking in front of the Administration Building. Freshmen were banned from parking their cars on University Avenue and were warned to attend chapel every day.

It was very different across town at what was called Southern Campus. This school began life as a branch of the State Normal School and, in 1919, became part of the University of California in which it was south to Berkeley's north. At UCLA—that's what it was called after 1924—there was no worry about freshmen parking since most students weren't lucky enough to have autos and depended instead upon streetcars. The L.A. Railway's Yellow "V" (for Vermont) car came

Above. USC meets UCLA at their common home field, the Coliseum, 1939. Within three years, the rivalry had been firmly established and it was unthinkable that a football season could end without a struggle between Troy and the Bruins.

Below. A loyal Trojan booster, ca. the early 1930s.

as close as a mile from campus. Frats and sororities were in the background. Men favored sweater vests, women long skirts and nobody cared about bobbed hair. There was some interest, however, in football.

Nineteen men turned out for the first football practice, and the team formed from them lost its first game to Manual Arts, a high school, by the lopsided score of 73-0. It wasn't until 1927 that the team, coached by Bill Spaulding, was deemed fit for admission to the PCC, and it was another two years before UCLA upset Montana, 14-0, for its first conference victory.

In 1927 and 1928, UCLA played USC. The match up was a natural but unequal. USC won both games by scores of 76-0 and 52-0. Regretfully, further pairings were set aside.

In 1936, the two teams were once again set against one another and the entire city eagerly awaited the outcome. The UCLA Bruins were favored. It was a defensive battle all the way before a crowd of 100,000 at the Coliseum. There were six fumbles in the game, five of which UCLA recovered. But, at the final gun, the score was tied 7-7. A small riot followed as players fought for the game ball. Actor Joe E. Brown, a big UCLA fan, got the ball, had it suitably mounted and it became the trophy presented to the victor in the annual contest.

Next year's game was witnessed by 103,000 fans who saw USC dominate. Late in the game, UCLA quarterback Kenny Washington let fly a pass that traveled sixty-two yards in the air, part of a UCLA drive which ultimately came up short. But it was the 1939 game that offered the greatest excitement since, for the first time in its history, UCLA had a chance for the Rose Bowl. All they had to do was beat USC. The UCLA backfield was phenomenal, composed of Jackie Robinson, Woody Strode and Kenny Washington. But getting past USC is never easy and, after a grinding defensive battle, the game ended in a scoreless tie, knocking UCLA out of the roses. In a few short years, the UCLA-USC rivalry had been established as one of the greatest in the nation.

The 1932 Olympics. The greatest sporting event of the age was the 1932 Olympics, hand-delivered to Los Angeles by real estate magnate and civic booster William May Garland. Garland, the story goes, was traveling in Europe and happened across the 1920 Antwerp Games. He was impressed by the pageantry and was convinced the Olympic movement could benefit by coming to Los Angeles. And certainly there was much to be said for hosting the Games by publicity conscious L.A.

In the early 1920s, Los Angeles was awarded the 1932 Games, to be the Tenth Modern Olympiad. Of course, by the time the Games had opened, much had happened in the world, chiefly the Depression. A number of cost-cutting and cost-saving measures tempered traditional Olympic extravagance. The police force was prevailed upon by Chief Steckel to work twelve-hour instead of eight-hour days and to cancel all vacations. UCLA and USC students were hired as temporary police officers, handling traffic. One thing the Committee didn't do was sell souvenirs. "The official Olympic Committee," announced chairman Zack Farmer, "has endorsed no stamp, novelty, letterhead, car ornament or any other article for sale."

Los Angeles' most famous economy, wildly successful, was the construction of an Olympic Village. At first, the idea was opposed by nations who believed too much familiarity bred contempt and led to the theft of training secrets. Grudgingly, the concept was accepted.

The Village rose in Baldwin Hills, cottages each housing four athletes assembled at the rate of fifty a day. The resulting small city housed 2,000 athletes and trainers with everything from laundries to thirty-one dining halls. Woman were not allowed within the confines of the Village so as not to disturb the equanimity of the Olympians. Lady athletes were housed in a downtown hotel.

Tickets for the Games were priced with due regard to the prevailing economic climate. Opening and closing days were tops at $3, boxing was $1 and $2, weight lifting 50¢ and $1, and no tickets were required for the equestrian events, or

The opening of the 1932 Los Angeles Olympics.

One of the official Olympic billboards. The Olympic emblem sold for 50¢ which went to the support of the U.S. Olympic Team. It was the only authorized Olympic souvenir.

the marathon, shooting, cross-country, yachting, 50,000-meter walk, and the road cycling events. Attendance was high and the Games were profitable. In fact, it was the only time in history the Games were profitable.

Opening ceremonies were held Sunday, July 30, 1932, and Los Angeles was delighted with the long-promised spectacle at last here. There were, of course, some minor disappointments. The great Paavo Nurmi was not in attendance, having been disqualified for professionalism. The Argentines sent two teams which promptly got into fisticuffs with one another. Actually, they *were* expected to do well in boxing. The French repeatedly grumbled about American Prohibition which denied them an element vital to their training table: wine. They were reduced to using sugar syrup. Manchukuo, the puppet Japanese state, was refused admission. But the application inspired the Chinese, who had not intended on fielding a team, to make a token entry. One sprinter represented China. He did not win a medal.

There was concern that Los Angeles' fabled summer sun would be too much for some athletes. The Olympic Committee promised to supply entrants with an official weather projection a year ahead of time. Unfortunately, the period selected to represent the average temperature turned out to be a heat wave. This information was quickly suppressed. Happily, the weather for the Games was perfect.

The Japanese were the source of much fascination and not a little hostility owing to the recent outbreak of war in China. They were expected to dominate the swimming events and they did, with the exception of the 400 meters freestyle which was won, to great national applause, by Clarence Crabbe, later and better known as Buster Crabbe.

Ralph Metcalfe of Marquette was favored in the 100 meters but, in a thrilling, close finish, another American, scrappy Eddie Tolan, edged him out. Tolan went on to win the 200 meters as well. A new world or Olympic record was set in every men's running event from 100 meters to 10,000 except for the 3,000-meter steeplechase. Owing to a confused official's mistake, that race included an extra lap.

The hero, or heroine, of the Games was Mildred "Babe" Didrickson who weighed 128 pounds and hailed from Texas. She was undeniably one of the great women athletes of all time. She won the 80 meters and then the high jump. But this victory was taken away and her ranking put down to second because of her unorthodox style under a rule repealed a year later. Then, in the javelin toss, pitted against the world record holder, Babe casually tossed the stick ten feet past the previous high mark. Amazed observers reported that Babe's throw had practically no arc to it and, had she lifted the javelin, it might have gone even further.

The 1932 Olympics were a smashing success. The only man who might have enjoyed attending and who did not was President Herbert Hoover, who thought the Games needlessly frivolous in hard economic times. He violated long-standing Olympic tradition by becoming the first head of state of the host nation not to appear in person to open the Games. He pleaded the demands of his heated campaign with FDR in sending Vice President Charles Curtis. Those associated with the Olympics movement were sure Hoover was cursed. And sure enough, he lost.

INDEX

Agua Caliente, 100–101; Open 100
Ah Tom, *See* Gubbins, Tom
Albori, Marco, 47, 51
Alexandria Hotel, 112–113
Alguin, "Little Phil," 49
All-Year Club, 19–20, 21
Alpine Tavern, 23
Ambassador Hotel, 112
American Broadcasting
    Corporation, 74
Angelus Temple, 96, 97
Animal farms, 85–87
Anthony, Earle C., 25–26
Anti-Saloon League, 57
Arbuckle, Fatty, 22, 80, 121
Arizona, 81
Armstrong, Henry, 123
Ascot Speedway, 118
Astaire, Fred, 103
Avalon, 101–104

Banning brothers, 101–103
Banning, Phineas, 101
Bara, Theda, 80
Barratry, 62
Baseball, 119–120
Battalino, Bat, 122
Baum, L. Frank, 17
Beaches, 27
Bel-Air (Calif.), 35, 83
Bell, Alphonzo E., 33–35
Berman, Jacob, 40–43
Bernhardt, Sarah, 105
Berry, Leonora King, 80
Better America Foundation, 42
Beverly Hills Hotel, 35
Biltmore Hotel, 100, 118
Bing Kong tong, 89–90
Blake, George, 121–122, 123
Bledsoe, Benjamin, 49
"Blockade system," 50
Blondeau, Mrs., 74
Bob Shuler's Magazine, 50
Boddy, Manchester, 10
Boone, Ike, 120
Boos, Cyrus, 110

Boos, Henry, 110
Boos, Horace, 110–111
Boos, John, 110
Bootleggers, 34, 60–62
Bootleg Highway, 60
Bostock, Fred C., 85
Bowron, Fletcher, 55
Boxing, 58, 120–123
Brand, Leslie C., 17
Brandon, Richard, 78
Briegleb, Rev. Gustave, 52, 53,
    62–63
Brinkley, Dr. J. R., 22
Brown Derby, the, 75–76, 79
Brown, Forman, 78
Bruins, 127
"Bucket shops," 40
Bum Blockade, 20–21
Bunion Derby, the, 118–119
Burnett, Harry, 78

Cafeterias, 83–84, 109–112
Cain, Paul, 66
California Alligator Farm, 87
Californio, 7
Cardenas, Pres. (of Mexico), 101
Caress, Ezekiel, 47
Carr, Harry, 20, 93
Casinos, floating, 61, 65–71
Casting, film, 84–85
Cawston's Ostrich Farm, 87
Central Casting, 84–85
Chandler, Harry, 19, 38, 49, 92
Chandler, Raymond, 66
Chaplin, Charlie, 80, 121
Chapman, C. C., 35
Chasen, Dave, 75
Chicago American, 80
Chicago Bears, 118
Chicago Cubs, 103
China City, 93
Chinatown, 85, 89–93;
    gambling in, 90–91
City of Panama, 66
Clark, Dave, 54
Clark, William Andrews, 7

Clifton's, 54; Brookdale, 112;
    South Seas, 111–112
Clinton, Clifford, 54–55, 111–112
Club Montmartre, 75, 114
Cobb, Bob, 75–76
Coffroth, Sunny Jim, 99–100
Collins, Walter, 51–52
Corbitt, Gentleman Jim, 120
Cornero, Frank, 60, 62
Cornero, Tony, 60–62, 66–71
Crabbe, Buster, 129
Crawford, Charles Henry, 45–54
Critic of Critics, The, 53–54
Cross, W. Simson, 85
Cryer, Charles, 46–50
Culver City, 15, 59, 75, 85, 113
Culver, Harry, 15–16, 85
Curtis, Charles, 129

Daily News, 9–11, 29, 60, 66, 79,
    81, 83
Davis, James Edgar, 20–21, 49–50,
    51, 55, 90
Davies, Marion, 81–83
De Mille, Cecil B., 42, 74, 80, 93
Depression, 76, 97, 114, 115, 123, 127
Di Ciolla, Dominic, 60
Didrickson, Mildred "Babe," 129
Dietrich, Marlene, 79
Doheny, E. L., 31
Donnarsari, 61
Doyle, Jack, 58, 60, 119, 120–121
Drury, Morley, 124–125
Duffy, Henry, 76
Dundee, Johnny, 120–121

Echo Park, 96
Egyptian Theater, 75
El Capitan, 76
El Monte (Calif.), 85
"Encyclopedia lots," 9
Evans, Dr. W. A., 59
Everington, Col. W., 47
Examiner, 9, 43, 80
Express, 121

Fairbanks, Douglas, 80, 81
Falcon Lair, 81
Farewell, My Lovely, 66
Farmer, Jack, 127
Farming, 17, 20; anthrax
    outbreak, 20
Fast One, 66
Federal Bureau of Investigation
    (FBI), 38, 39, 40, 61
Federal Communication Corporation
    (FCC), 53
Federal Radio Commission (FRC),
    53, 54
Film industry, 73–87, 92
Fitts, Buron, 69
Flint, Motley, 42
Flintridge, 42
Follow the Fleet, 79
Football: college, 123–127;
    pro, 117–118
Ford, John Anson, 54
Foreign Club, 100
Four Corners Cafe, 34
Foursquare Gospel, 96, 97

Gable, Clark, 79
Gambling, 65–71, 90–91, 100–101;
    on ships, 61, 66–71
Gans, Bob, 47
Gans, Joe, 47
Garbo, Greta, 79
Garcia, Ceferino, 123
Garland, William May, 127
Gay, Charles, 85–87
Gay's Lion Farm, 85–87
Genaro, Frankie, 121–122
Getzoff, Ben, 43
Gillette, E. S., 68
Glaze, H. F., 90
Glendale (Calif.), 17
Golden Age, the, 77
Golf, 100, 117
Goodman, Benny, 105
Grange, Harold, 118
Grauman's Chinese Theater, 75
Grauman, Sid, 75

Greenacres, 81
Grey, Ralph, 55
Griffith, D. W., 73, 74
Gubbins, Tom (Ah Tom), 91–92

Halas, George, 118
Haldeman, Harry, 42
Hamer, S. H., 62
Hays, Will, 80
Hearst, William Randolph, 61, 81–82
Heath, Lee, 114
Henderson, Gus, 123–124
Hertz, Alfred, 76
Hollywood (Calif.), 9, 17, 73–87
Hollywood Bowl, 7, 76–77, 79
Hollywood Playhouse, 76
Hollywood Stars, 120
Holy Roller Pentacostalism, 95–97
Home, George, 23–24
Hoover, Herbert, 129
Hoover, J. Edgar, 39, 55, 61
Hop Sing tong, 89–90
Horse racing, 99–101
Horsley, David, 74
Hotel St. Catherine, 103
Hudkins, Ace, 122
Hughes, Howard, 103–104
Huntington Beach, 31–32

Internal Revenue Service (IRS),
   61–62
Island Villa, 101
It Happened One Night, 79

Jackson, Helen Hunt, 104
Jacobsen, Carl, 52
Jazz Singer, The, 74
Jeffries, Jim, 100, 120
Johanna Smith, 65–66
Joke Wah Ming Company, 91
Jolson, Al, 104
Jones, Charles A., 47
Jones, Howard, 124–125
Julian, Chauncey C., 36–43
Julian Petroleum Company
   (Julian Pete), 37–43

Keno, 90
Keyes, Asa, 42, 43, 97
Keystone Kops, 73, 74, 121
KFSG, 97
KGEF, 50
Kinney, Abbot, 104–106
Klondyke Cafe, 101–103
Knights of Columbus, 50
Kynette, Earl, 21, 55

La Barba, Fidel, 121–122
Laemmle, Carl, 74
Lane, Bill, 120
Langan, John, 21
Langdon, Harry, 15, 81
Lasky, Jesse, 74, 81
Leadville (Calif.), 41
Lem Gooey Fong, 90
Leonis, John, 58
Levy, Al, 115
Lewis Petroleum, 40
Lewis, S. C., 40–43
Lick, James, 101
Lincoln Highway, 13
Lions, 85–87; Leo, 85; Numa,
   85–87; Slats, 85–87
Lloyd, Harold, 81
Long, Baron, 100–101
Long Beach (Calif.), 32, 65–66
Los Angeles: and automobiles,
   24–26; beaches, 27; building
   boom, 9, 14–15; cafeterias, 83–84,
   109–112; climate, 19; clothing, 22,
   79; crime syndicates, 45–55; earth-
   quakes, 27–29; gastronomy, 91,
   109–115; newspapers, 9–11; New
   Year's Eve celebrations, 112–115;
   police department, 20–21, 45–55,
   90–91; population growth, 7,
   13–14; pronunciation of, 26–27;
   oil rush, 7, 31–43, 106; Olympics
   (1932), 51, 127–129; sports,
   117–129; streetcars, 17, 23–24,
   32, 58–59, 74, 106, 119, 126–127;
   traffic, 24–26
Los Angeles Angels, 119–120

Los Angeles Athletic Club, 121
Los Angeles Chamber of Commerce,
   17, 20, 81, 117
Los Angeles Open, 117
Los Angeles Philharmonic, 7, 76
Los Angeles Police Department
   (LAPD), 20–21, 45–55; Chinatown
   Detail, 90–91
Los Angeles Tigers, 118

Mack, Everett, 63
Mah jong, 90
Malibu, 83
Mankin, Thum, 62
Mayer, Louis B., 42, 73, 81
McAfee, Guy, 47, 52, 53–54, 55
McCarey, Uncle Tom, 59–60, 120
McPherson, Aimee Semple, 42,
   95–97
McWilliams, Carey, 110
Media Park, 15
Metropole, 101
Metropolitan Pictures, 73
MGM, 75, 85
Miller, Glenn, 105
Minter, Mary Miles, 80
Mix, Tom, 80
Monfalcone, 66
Monte Carlo, 66
Mosher, Helen, 110
Motor Car Dealers Association, 26
Mulholland, William, 20, 27, 29
Music Box, The, 76

National Psychological Institute, 22
Nestor Film Company, 74
New Chinatown, 93
New York Times, 9
Nick the Greek, 47
Normand, Mabel, 80, 121
Notre Dame, 124–126

Oaken, Ben, 61
Oakes, Louis D., 49, 63
Ocean Park (Calif.), 96, 105
Oil rush, 7, 31–43, 106; syndicates,

36–43
Ole's Inn, 41
Oleson, Otto K., 77–79
Olympic Auditorium, 121
Olympics, Los Angeles, 51, 127–129
Olympic Village, 127
Olvera Street project, 93
Opium, 89
Ormister, Kenneth, 97

Pacific Coast Conference (PCC), 123
Pacific Coast League (PCL), 119
Pacific Electric, 17, 23–24, 32,
   58–59, 74, 106, 119, 126–127
Pai gow, 90
Pantages, Alexander, 50
Pantages, Lois, 50
Parrot, Kent Kane, 46–47, 49
Pendergast, Lyle, 63; machine, 45
Phillips, Armour, 9
Pickfair, 81
Pickford, Mary, 80, 81
Pico, Pio, 101
Pike, Milton, 43
Pink Rat, the, 62–63
Polo, 117
Porter, John, 51, 54
Pot Boiler Art Theater, 76
Premzyl, 61–62
Press, A. E., 22
Price Waterhouse, 39
Prohibition, 24, 34, 57–63, 99–100,
   101, 113–114, 115, 129; price of
   liquor during, 62; Prohibition
   Party, 57
Pyle, C. C., 117–119

Ramona, 79
Randall, Charles, 57
Raymond, Harry, 54–55, 106
Real estate boom, 15–17
Reid, Wallace, 80
Rex, 67–71
Rivers, Joe, 120–121
Roach, Hal, 75, 85, 117
Robbins, Thomas, 101

Rockne, Knute, 124–125
Rodin, Gil, 105
Rogers, Ginger, 79
Rogers, Will, 117
Romanoff, Mike, 75
Rose Bowl, 113, 123–124
Rothwell, Walter, 76
Royal Dutch Shell, 32
Runyon, Damon, 118

San Simeon, 61
Santa Anita Race Track, 101
Santa Catalina Island (Calif.), 99,
    101–104; Casino, 103–104
Santa Fe Railroad, 32, 92–93
Santa Fe Springs (Calif.), 32–38
Santa Monica bay, 69–71
Santa Monica Evening Outlook,
    67–68
Sardinias, Eligio (Kid Chocolate), 122
Sartori, J. F., 40
Sasso, Augustus, 47
Scout, Dick, 60
Security Bank, 40
Selig, Col. William, 73
Selig Zoo, 73, 87
Selznick International, 75, 85
Sennett, Mack, 73, 121
Shatto, George, 101
Shaw, Frank, 54, 55, 69
Shaw, Joe, 54
Shelton, Ralph, 60
Ship Cafe, 58, 100, 105
Shippey, Lee, 75
Showboat, 66, 70
Shuler, Rev. Bob, 49, 50–53, 54,
    63, 85, 97
Sierra Club, 111
Signal Hill, 32, 35
Sinclair, Upton, 49
Smuggling, 60–62, 66, 101
Snyder, Meredith "Pinky," 46
Soo Ho Long, 90
Soo Hoo, Peter, 93
Southern Pacific Railroad, 13, 92–93
South, Walter, 60

Southwest Blue Book, 80–81
Spencer, Herb, 53–54
Squaw Man, The, 74
Standard Oil, 31–32
Stanford, 71, 124
Statz, Arnold "Jigger," 120
Steckel, Dick, 47, 51, 54, 90, 127
Sterling, Christine, 93
Streetcars, 17, 23–24, 32, 58–59, 74,
    106, 119, 126–127
Studios, film, 83–84; cafeterias,
    83–84
Swanson, Gloria, 81

Tango, 67, 70
Taxis, water, 68, 69
Taylor, William Desmond, 80
Teagarden, Jack, 105
Texas, 66, 70
Thirty Years Among the Dead, 22
Tijuana, 99; Race Track, 99–100
Times, 9–10, 14, 19, 26–27, 43, 53,
    59, 63, 65–66, 75, 80, 92, 109
Tolan, Eddie, 129
Tong wars, 89–90
Toplitzky, Joe, 42
Traffic, 25–26
Trinity Methodist Church South,
    50, 85
Trojans, 124–126
Tse-far, 90

Universal City, 74
University of California, Berkeley
    (Cal), 7, 123–127
University of California, Los Angeles
    (UCLA), 7, 126–127
University of Southern California
    (USC), 7, 46, 123–127

Valentino, Rudolph, 75, 81, 100
Vanderbilt, Cornelius, 9–10
Van Nuys, I. N., 15
Van Nuys (Calif.), 17
Venice-by-the-Sea (Calif.), 58, 99,
    104–106, 113; piers, 105–106

Venus, 100
Vernon (Calif.), 58, 120–121
Vernon Country Club, 50, 58,
    63, 100
Vernon Tigers, 119–120
Vine Street Theater, 76
Vitagraph, 74
Vollmer, August, 49
Von KleinSmid, Rufus, 53

Walker, Mickey, 122
Warner Bros., 74
Warren, Earl, 70–71
Wayne, John, 80–81
Weinstock, Matt, 10, 19, 22
Western Lead Mines and
    Western Lead, 41
Westlake Presbyterian Church, 63
Whitsett, W. P., 16–17
Wickland, Carl A., 22
Wiggins, Hank, 20
Wilson, George, 118
Windsor (Calif.), 59
Wong Fong, 90
Woodill, Gilbert, 26
Wright Act, 63
Wright, Willard Huntington, 109
Wrigley, William, 103–104
Wrigley, William, Jr., 104

Yale Puppeteers, 78
Young, Clara Kimball, 26
Young, Loretta, 79